IMAGES
of Sport

LEEDS UNITED
IN EUROPE

UNITED'S EURO DAZZLERS SMASH CLUB RECORD

Bowyer keeping his feet on floor

MAN-OF-THE-MATCH Lee Bowyer was keeping his feet firmly on the ground after steering Leeds United to their emphatic victory last night.

Bowyer's double strike earned him rave reviews and once again left many observers wondering why he has still to break into Kevin Keegan's full England squad.

But the young midfielder preferred to talk about his United team mates and their chances of success, rather than any personal triumphs.

Clutching his man-of-the-match bottle of champagne, Bowyer *(pictured)* said: "I'm not surprised we won so convincingly because we played so very well.

"It looked like we could have scored a lot more goals, so it should be interesting when we go to Moscow. They will have to push up and we have good prospects of getting a similar result.

"It's going to be tough over in Moscow. It will be very cold and we are not really used to those conditions, but I'm confident we'll get the right result."

The former Charlton star added: "To be honest I don't think I am playing as well as I did last season because I have had a lot of problems with my groins. I know that when I wake up in the morning I'll be sore.

"I had a bad game on Saturday, but I really needed to play. I seem to be losing the ball quite a lot and that is because you need to train all the time – I am not doing that at the moment.

"Hopefully we can win something, but there is still a long way to go. You can't start thinking at this stage that we're going to win this and win that."

BY PHIL ROSTRON

TEN out of ten. Excellent. Leeds United passed their European examination with distinction last night and, in the process, lowered a 68-year club record of consecutive victories.

Their 4-1 UEFA Cup second round first leg defeat of Lokomotiv Moscow surpassed the wildest of dreams and set Elland Road alight as United waltzed to a breathtaking tenth successive victory in all competitions.

The second leg in Moscow on November 4 was reduced to a formality and United manager David O'Leary said: "If we go through, and it would be nice to think that we might from this base, it would be good to be rewarded with a nice easy touch in the third round."

Combative

United's success was based on blinding pace and high-lighted by a spectacular individual performance from Lee Bowyer, who once again made it very difficult for England boss Kevin Keegan to ignore him when he sits down to pick the squad for the two Euro 2000 qualifiers against Scotland.

Bowyer netted two fine goals, never shirked an issue and was combative from first whistle to last. If Keegan believes he has seen better and has someone else in mind then he is in a world of his own.

Said O'Leary: "It was a great win against a dangerous team. We needed this kind of cushion going to Moscow because they are a fine side. If somebody had offered 1-0 before the match I would have taken it.

"We acquired a lucky tag against Sheffield Wednesday in the league on Saturday, so maybe ten out of ten is lucky. But nobody mentions Manchester United, when we played them off the pitch at Old Trafford and they took two chances in the last ten minutes. Nobody said to me afterwards that we had been robbed.

"We are not going to play, week in week out, great football. Sometimes you just get lucky.

"Foreign team such as Lokomotiv ask questions of you. I learned in 20 years at Arsenal that if you don't concentrate you get punished and that happened tonight with a free kick which, I believe, should not have been given anyway.

"At this stage last season against Roma we went out because we didn't take our chances. We hit the post a couple of times, but here we were more clinical with our finishing.

"We wanted to set the tempo in the knowledge that they are very quick on the break."

Asked by a Russian observer why Leeds didn't play in a familiar British style, O'Leary quipped: "Because I'm Irish!"

"I thought we did well, playing good football, trying to excite and going out to score goals. I still think that our best display of the season was at Old Trafford. We didn't get anything out of it but that is this silly game of football which we play."

● UNITED midfielder Bruno Ribeiro is to hold talks with Sheffield United today regarding a £500,000 switch to Bramall Lane.

MATCH report – pages 60 & 61

UNITED'S GREAT EURO NIGHTS

● In 1968 Leeds go to Hungary for a Fairs Cup Final second leg against Ferencvaros holding a 1-0 advantage from the first leg. A goalless draw gives them the trophy.

● In 1971 they win the trophy again, this time at Elland Road against Juventus. A 2-2 draw in Italy is followed by a 1-1 home draw and Leeds triumph on away goals.

● In 1975 Leeds beat Barcelona 2-1 at Elland Road in the first leg of the European Cup semi-final. A 1-1 draw in Spain takes them to a Paris final against Bayern Munich, who win 2-0.

● In the 1973 Cup Winners Cup final in Salonika they press AC Milan all the way but lose 1-0.

● In their 1968 Fairs Cup run Leeds travel to Spora Luxembourg in the first round first leg and win 9-0. It's only 7-0 in the return at Elland Road.

● United dish out a 4-1 hammering to Lokomotiv Moscow in a UEFA Cup tie at Elland Road in October 1999.

TEN OF THE BEST

LUCAS RADEBE WRITES FOR THE YEP – SEE PAGE 61

The *Yorkshire Evening Post* report on Leeds achieving a club record tenth successive victory following their 4-1 triumph over Lokomotiv Moscow in the UEFA Cup, 22 October 1999.

IMAGES
of Sport

LEEDS UNITED
IN EUROPE

Compiled by
David Saffer and Howard Dapin

This book is dedicated to our fathers, Harold Saffer
and Syd Dapin, for taking us to our first games.

TEMPUS

First published 2000
Copyright © David Saffer and Howard Dapin, 2000

Tempus Publishing Limited
The Mill, Brimscombe Port,
Stroud, Gloucestershire, GL5 2QG

ISBN 0 7524 2043 7

Typesetting and origination by
Tempus Publishing Limited
Printed in Great Britain by
Midway Clark Printing, Wiltshire

Cover picture: Harry Kewell in action against AS Roma, 9 March 2000.

Also available from Tempus Publishing

Contents

Mick Jones made 42 appearances in Europe for Leeds, scoring 17 times. His goals include a club record 8 in the European Cup. Mick played in three European Finals: 1968, 1971 and 1973.

I struggled at first when I joined Leeds, it took me a while to settle down and I found it difficult to find the net. As the pressure built I was fortunate to make my European debut against part-timers Spora in Luxembourg, and scored my first goal for the club. The goal settled my nerves and I then began to score on a regular basis.

Looking back, the highlight for me in Europe has to be the goal I scored against Ferencvaros in the '68 Final. It wasn't a classic but it meant so much to so many. The thing I remember most vividly about that match was Gary Sprake's unbelievable performance in the return in Budapest. He was outstanding. Some of the saves he pulled off were incredible. He won us the Cup that night.

European nights were extra special and had a unique atmosphere. The team loved going away. Away crowds always tried to intimidate us – they failed, it just brought the best out of us. For years it seemed that we were in Europe every week, playing one side or another. Without a doubt European football was different to the domestic game, the teams we played were either really poor or incredibly skilful, and obviously the further we went in a tournament the harder the matches became.

The boys have brought back many wonderful memories for me, I am sure you will enjoy the book.

Mick Jones

Paul Madeley played in the club's first match in Europe in 1965 and, amazingly, played his last in 1979. In all he made 70 European appearances, scoring 4 times, and appeared in every European final except for 1967.

I remember the '71 Final as if it was yesterday. The first match in Turin was abandoned just after half-time, but really it should never have started because torrential rain had fallen before the game and there were huge pools of water all over the pitch.

Two days later the pitch was soft but definitely playable. I remember all my goals as I didn't get that many. It's funny that Mick Bates and I were the ones to score that night because neither of us were renowned for goal scoring. Mine was from outside the penalty box. The bench were looking for me to pass the ball wide but I decided to have a go. As I hit it a defender ran across me and the ball just clipped his heel; the goalkeeper was committed to going across the shot and the ball squirmed across him and just inside the post to the other corner. The 2-2 score was a great result and we really fancied our chances at home. I got injured in the return and only played about half an hour. I was really annoyed to miss the celebrations on the pitch at the end.

The major disappointments for me in Europe were the final defeats in '73 and '75. Much has been said about the refereeing in those matches, but for me neither Milan nor Bayern came out with any honour winning in those circumstances. Nevertheless, I loved playing in Europe.

I know David and Howard have worked hard documenting this story, I know you'll be impressed by the finished product.

Paul Madeley

David Saffer

Howard Dapin

Introduction

European football was a distant dream when Don Revie became manager in 1961. In his first season in charge the club was struggling to achieve mediocrity – opponents such as Leyton Orient, Scunthorpe and Plymouth Argyle were proving difficult to beat. Revie's single aim then was to avoid relegation to Division Three, which was only just achieved. Despite this inauspicious start, he was inspired by Europe's finest and remained totally focused on bringing these teams back to Elland Road.

Revie set about changing fundamental beliefs, traditions and everyday events at the club to achieve this. He brought in new training and coaching techniques, he insisted his team travelled first class and most controversially dropped the traditional blue and gold club colours for the all-white of Real Madrid, the then five-time winners of the European Cup. Revie was adamant in his belief that one day Leeds United would compete on an equal footing with the Spanish giants.

Revie blended talented youngsters such as Billy Bremner, Norman Hunter and Paul Reaney, with players of the calibre of Bobby Collins and Alan Peacock. The new philosophy worked. His team clinched the Division Two title in 1964 and in a remarkable first season in the top flight finished runners-up in both League and FA Cup; his team had qualified for Europe.

A new chapter in the Leeds United story began on 29 September 1965 when Italian giants Torino visited Elland Road. Since that date the club's supporters have witnessed the highs and lows that only European football can produce. Notable victories over the best teams in Europe such as Barcelona, Valencia, Roma, Ferencvaros and Juventus remain clear in the memory, as do those matches we'd rather forget.

As we approach a new European season, and participation in the Champions League for the first time, David O'Leary's youngsters have begun to re-establish the club as a European force. It will surely not be long before Leeds United are illuminating the European stage to the same intensity that Revie's Leeds achieved. So as we head into the future we recall the past.

Enjoy the memories.

David Saffer and Howard Dapin, June 2000

One
Stepping Out
1965-1967

Leeds United's 1965/66 squad which took part in the club's first European campaign. From left to right, back row: Willie Bell, Paul Reaney, Peter Lorimer, Rod Belfitt, Terry Cooper. Middle row: Bobby Collins (captain), Norman Hunter, Brian Williamson, Gary Sprake, Jimmy Greenhoff, Paul Madeley. Front row: Rod Johnson, Jim Storrie, Jack Charlton, Alan Peacock, Billy Bremner, Johnny Giles, Albert Johanneson.

Consolidation is the prediction in the 1964/65 pre-season handbook; a desire echoed in Speed's cartoon. Nobody wanted to place too great an expectancy on the players. Leeds however performed incredibly, finishing runners-up in both League and FA Cup – European qualification had been achieved.

On 29 September 1965 Leeds United played their first ever European match, against Italian giants Torino. This is the editorial from the match programme in which United welcome their guests. In an attempt to outfox the Italian man-markers, Revie switched his forwards around and gave them different numbered shirts to those which they usually wore. Despite the success of this ploy all Leeds had to show for their first half domination was a solitary Bremner strike after twenty-five minutes.

Peacock heads home past Torino 'keeper Vieri for United's second goal. Leeds then showed their inexperience by chasing a third, Torino scoring on the break with just minutes remaining. In the return Leeds put on an outstanding defensive display, overcoming the loss of Collins with a fractured right thigh after fifty minutes. They held out for a 0-0 draw and a 2-1 aggregate win.

LEEDS UNITED A.F.C. LTD.

Registered Office and Ground : E L L A N D R O A D
Telephone 7-6037/8   Telegrams " Football, Leeds "
President :
The Right Hon. THE EARL OF HAREWOOD, LL.D.
Life Vice-Presidents :
JOHN H. BROMLEY, Esq.   S. L. BLENKINSOP, Esq.
Directors
H. L. REYNOLDS, Esq., Chairman   A. MORRIS, Esq.
Ald. P. A. WOODWARD,   R. R. ROBERTS, Esq.
          Vice-Chairman   S. G. SIMON, Esq.
S. BOLTON, Esq.   Team Manager : D. REVIE
M. CUSSINS, Esq.   General Manager and Secretary :
H. A. MARJASON, Esq.   C. J. WILLIAMSON, F.I.A.C.

WEDNESDAY, 29th SEPTEMBER, 1965

BENVENUTO TORINO !

Siamo fieri di accogliere la Torino a Leeds in quest' unica occasione nella storia della nostra squadra—il nostra debutto nel football Europeo per mezzo dell' "Inter-City Fairs Cup."

E un vero onore per noi prendere parte in questa nuova forma di football in un incontro con una squadra così distinta e famosa proveniente da Torino, una delle più importanti sedi del giuoco del calcio in Italia.

Come noi, anche loro, hanno appena mancato l'onore di essere in testa, la stagione scorsa, trovandosi—loro terzi, noi secondi. Per la Coppa, sono stati battuti nella semi-finale, mentre noi abbiamo perduto la finale.

Siamo sicuri che questo match sarà memorabile e che le due squadre saranno orgogliose di averlo reso tale.

This is what we said in Italian above to our Torino friends

WELCOME TO TORINO !

We offer Torino a warm welcome to Leeds on this unique occasion in our history—our debut in competitive European football through the medium of the Inter-City Fairs Cup.

We are delighted to enter this new form of football against such distinguished and accomplished visitors from Italy, one of the great homes of the game, as Torino.

Like ourselves they just missed top honours last season, being third in their national league while we were second in ours, and being beaten in the semi-final of their Cup while we lost the final of ours.

We look forward to a memorable match with both sides giving their best.

United faced SC Leipzig in the next round. Their 2-1 victory in East Germany was followed by a dour 0-0 draw. Here, Weigang makes a flying save to deny Bremner's goalbound effort at a snowbound Elland Road. Revie quickly developed a game plan in away legs. He instructed his side to silence the crowd by dominating the game early on. His belief was that if you frustrated the opposition, home supporters would soon turn against their own team, undermining their own players' confidence.

In a volatile fourth round clash at Elland Road on 2 February 1966, United came from behind to draw 1-1 with Valencia. With fifteen minutes remaining, and Leeds searching for a winner, the game erupted. 'Big Jack' was so incensed by the constant physical battering he was receiving, that he chased the Valencia 'keeper towards the corner flag. Here, the linesman and police restrain Jack. The referee took both teams off the pitch to calm down. Eleven minutes later the game resumed without Charlton and Ridagany. Within minutes Sanchez-Lage followed for hacking down Storrie. A war of words began after the game and a new referee was appointed for the return. Thankfully there was no bloodbath as Leeds displayed their growing maturity, soaking up everything the Spaniards could throw at them before silencing the crowd with a brilliant O'Grady strike to clinch another 2-1 aggregate win.

In United's 4-1 quarter-final victory over Ujpest Dozsa an unexpected visitor held play up for ten minutes. Neither Ujpest centre half Csordas nor a member of United's ground staff could tempt the four-legged visitor off the pitch. Leeds completed their victory over the Hungarians after a 1-1 draw behind the Iron Curtain.

The match programme from the Ujpest Dozsa clash at Elland Road, 2 March 1966.

OFFICIAL TOKEN

LEEDS UNITED F.C.
Ujpesti S.C.
34
1965 - 66

LEEDS UNITED AFC

Photograph by courtesy of the "Yorkshire Evening Post"   Price 6d.
versus
Ujpesti S.C.   N° 24694
WEDNESDAY, 2nd MARCH, 1966

The first leg of the semi-final was played in Spain and Leeds were subjected to brutal treatment by Real Zaragoza. Eventually Giles retaliated to constant provocation and was sent off five minutes from time. After losing by a single goal United levelled the aggregate score at 2-2 in the return leg with this header from Charlton.

Away goals counted for nothing in the 1965/66 season and in the play-off at Elland Road, Zaragoza ensured the irrelevance of United's home advantage with a stunning 3-1 triumph, their goals all coming in the opening fifteen minutes. Here, Marcelino threads the ball past Charlton, Sprake, Bremner and Reaney to open the scoring on 11 May 1966.

Leeds United's 1966/67 squad. From left to right, back row: Don Revie (manager), Alan Peacock, Willie Bell, Jack Charlton, Gary Sprake, Paul Madeley, Norman Hunter, Rod Belfitt, Les Cocker (trainer). Front row: Terry Cooper, Paul Reaney, Albert Johanneson, Billy Bremner (captain), Jimmy Greenhoff, Johnny Giles, Peter Lorimer, Eddie Gray.

After a first leg bye, Amsterdam was United's first destination in 1966/67. An impressive 3-1 victory made the return leg a formality. Leeds turned on the style at Elland Road, scoring five, with Johanneson grabbing a hat-trick. Here, DWS Amsterdam 'keeper Schryvers is unable to keep out this Johanneson drive which opened the scoring.

LEEDS UNITED		VALENCIA
LEEDS UNITED ALL WHITE		**VALENCIA** Colours

LEEDS UNITED		VALENCIA

LEEDS UNITED
ALL WHITE

1. **SPRAKE, Gary**
   GOAL
2. **REANEY, Paul**
   RIGHT BACK
3. **BELL, Willie**
   LEFT BACK
4. **BREMNER, Billy**
   RIGHT HALF
5. **CHARLTON, Jack**
   CENTRE HALF
6. **HUNTER, Norman**
   LEFT HALF
7. **O'GRADY, Mike**
   OUTSIDE RIGHT
8. **LORIMER, Peter**
   INSIDE RIGHT
9. **GREENHOFF, Jim**
   CENTRE FORWARD
10. **GRAY, Eddie**
    INSIDE LEFT
11. **JOHANNESON, A.**
    OUTSIDE LEFT

Subs: HARVEY, David

Referee:
Hans-Joachim Weyland
Germany

Linesmen:
WILFRIED HILKER
Germany
(Red flag)

JOSEF HOFFMANN
Germany
(Yellow flag)

VALENCIA
Colours

1. **PESUDO**
   GOAL
2. **SOL**
   RIGHT BACK
3. **VIDEGANY**
   LEFT BACK
4. **ROBERTO**
   RIGHT HALF
5. **MESTRE**
   CENTRE HALF
6. **PAQUITO**
   LEFT HALF
7. **GUILLOT**
   OUTSIDE RIGHT
8. **WALDO**
   INSIDE RIGHT
9. **ANSOLA**
   CENTRE FORWARD
10. **POLI**
    INSIDE LEFT
11. **CLARAMUNT**
    OUTSIDE LEFT

Subs: ....

Leeds faced Valencia in the third round. As in the previous year the Spaniards achieved a 1-1 draw at Elland Road, but on this occasion there was no repeat of the ugly scenes that marred the previous seasons encounter. This is the team sheet in the match programme for the game, which was played on 18 January 1967.

Valencia 'keeper Pesudo gets down to block Cooper's goal-bound shot. The goalie's bravery led to him being carried off before the final whistle.

In front of 48,000 fanatical Spaniards on 8 February 1967, United silenced the passionate crowd with a brilliant display, winning 2-0. Here, Giles is pictured opening the scoring.

At the final whistle it was obvious to everyone what this result meant to Leeds. Here, Sprake and Bremner hug as they leave the field.

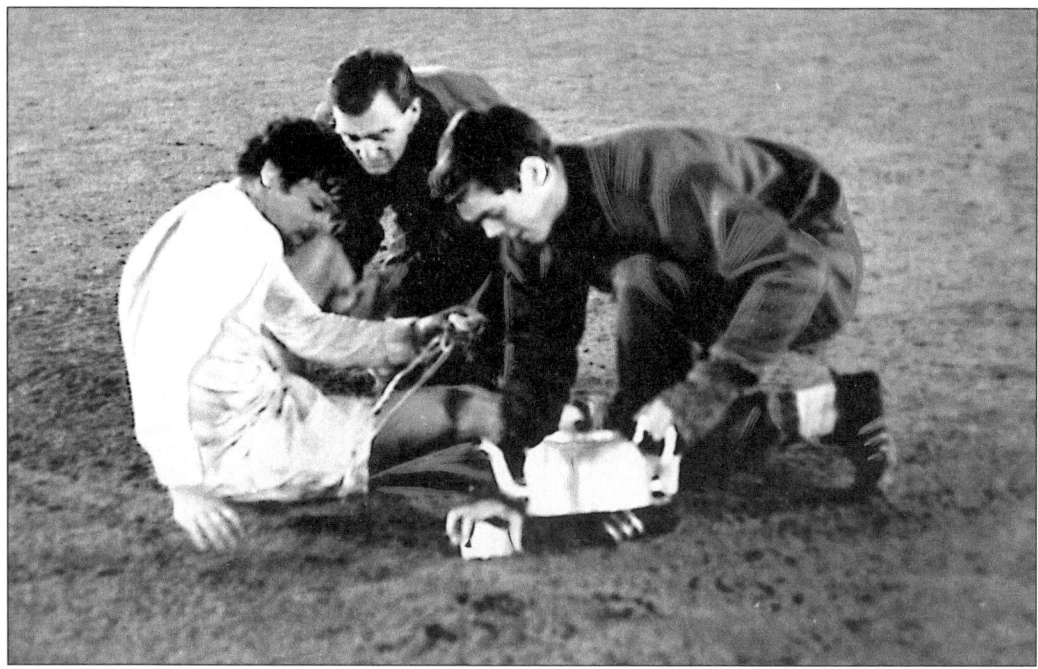

United's reward for defeating Valencia was a trip to Bologna in the quarter-finals. A 1-0 defeat in Italy was cancelled out by this Giles penalty in the return leg, taking the game into extra-time.

It seems bizarre that in the break before the start of the extra time period a hot cup of tea is the order of the day. Here, United's substitute 'keeper, a very young David Harvey, pours a cuppa for Eddie Gray whilst he receives treatment from trainer Les Cocker.

When he wasn't scoring goals, driving his team forward or unnerving the opposition with his tenacity, Billy Bremner also had the ability to choose correctly when the toss of a disc meant passage to the next round. Here, Revie, Sprake and Reaney congratulate him on his prediction.

In the semi-finals Leeds faced Scottish opposition. Kilmarnock, who had exceeded everybody's expectations by getting so far, gave United a real fright in the first leg at Elland Road on 19 May 1967. In an unbelievable opening half Leeds went into the break 4-2 ahead, Rod Belfitt scoring his first hat-trick for the club. This picture shows Belfitt sliding home his third goal. Unsurprisingly, the second period failed to match the first, with no addition to the score.

A solid defensive display by Leeds throughout a tense 0-0 draw in the return leg, played on 24 May 1967, ensured progress to the final. Here, eight Leeds players pack their area to keep their two-goal advantage intact.

In only their second season of European football Leeds had reached the final of the Inter-Cities Fairs Cup. Their opponents were the Yugoslavian team Dinamo Zagreb. The match was played at the start of the 1967/68 season when, unfortunately, Leeds were weakened by the loss of Bell, Madeley, Giles and Johanneson. United's makeshift side struggled throughout the first leg in Yugoslavia, losing 2-0 on 1 September 1967. Here, Charlton, Belfitt and Hunter challenge Dinamo 'keeper Skoric in one of the few attacks that the depleted United side managed.

The 1967 Fairs Cup final souvenir brochure.

How the teams lined up in the return leg as depicted in the match programme.

LEEDS UNITED		DINAMO ZAGREB
WHITE		BLUE
1. SPRAKE, Gary	Referee:	1. SKORIC
GOAL	SIGNOR SBARDELLA	GOAL
2. REANEY, Paul	Italy	2. GRACANIN
RIGHT BACK		RIGHT BACK
3. COOPER, Terry		3. BRNCIC
LEFT BACK		LEFT BACK
4. BREMNER, Billy		4. BELIN
RIGHT HALF		RIGHT HALF
5. CHARLTON, Jack		5. RAMLJAK
CENTRE HALF		CENTRE HALF
6. HUNTER, Norman		6. BLASKOVIC
LEFT HALF		LEFT HALF
7. LORIMER, Peter		7. CERCEK
OUTSIDE RIGHT		OUTSIDE RIGHT
8. GREENHOFF, Jim	Linesmen:	8. PIRIC
INSIDE RIGHT	SIGNOR CERNESE	INSIDE RIGHT
9. BELFITT, Rod	Italy	9. ZAMBATA
CENTRE FORWARD	(Red flag)	CENTRE FORWARD
10. GRAY, Eddie		10. GUCMIRTL
INSIDE LEFT		INSIDE LEFT
11. O'GRADY, Mike	SIGNOR DEROBBIO	11. RORA
OUTSIDE LEFT	Italy	OUTSIDE LEFT
Sub. HARVEY, David	(Yellow flag)	Subs. ....

The likelihood of Leeds overturning a two-goal deficit looked remote, particularly as in the five League games prior to the return Leeds had scored just three goals. However, United played with grit and determination, although in the end their constant attacks brought nothing but frustration. This image shows Belfitt beating Zagreb 'keeper Skoric with a header only to see his effort ruled out for an infringement. The Yugoslav's 2-0 aggregate victory was a bitter pill to swallow.

Two

From Luxembourg to Glasgow

1968-1970

Leeds United's first team squad, 1967/68. From left to right, back row: Norman Hunter, Alan Peacock, Jack Charlton, Paul Madeley, Eddie Gray, Rod Belfitt. Middle row: Don Revie (manager), Willie Bell, Mike O'Grady, David Harvey, Gary Sprake, Albert Johanneson, Rod Johnson, Jimmy Greenhoff. Front row: Paul Reaney, Bobby Collins, Johnny Giles, Billy Bremner (captain), Jim Storrie, Peter Lorimer, Terry Cooper.

Within weeks of being defeated finalists Leeds began their next campaign by thrashing CA Spora's team of part-timers from Luxembourg 9-0; United's biggest away triumph on foreign soil. A 7-0 thumping at Elland Road followed two weeks later. The goals were shared between Lorimer (5), Greenhoff (4), Johanneson (3), Bremner, Madeley, Jones and Cooper. Tougher opposition followed in the next round as United faced Partizan Belgrade, the Yugoslavian Army side. A 2-1 victory in Belgrade (above) was achieved by the teams' ability to chase and harass the opposition into mistakes. The return ended 1-1, United scraping through 3-2 on aggregate.

THE PATH TO THE FINAL

Eddie Gray, slamming the only goal of this third-round game against Hibs at Elland Road, took three of the Scottish defenders by surprise.

Two goals which spelt the end of the road for Hibs

Sprake lives up to his rating

ABOVE: United goalkeeper Gary Sprake foils Hibernian forward Stein, after the Scot had gone past Norman Hunter at Easter Road.

Centre-half Jack Charlton heads United into the quarter-final of the Fairs Cup with his late equaliser against Hibernian.

The hard-earned victory over Partizan earned United a tie against Hibernian, the unlikely conquerors of Napoli. The Scots had produced a remarkable performance in the previous round, overturning a 4-1 first leg deficit to win 6-4 on aggregate. Consequently, Leeds refused to underestimate their Scottish opponents. In the first leg at Elland Road, Gray gave Leeds a fourth minute lead, but a bone hard pitch made flowing football impossible and by the end Leeds were grateful for their slender advantage. In the return at Easter Road, Charlton's late header took United through 2-1 on aggregate. Once again the *Yorkshire Evening Post* captured the action.

25

In the quarter-finals Leeds faced Glasgow Rangers. The first leg at Ibrox was a sell-out. In a first for the club, fans were given the opportunity to watch a closed-circuit beam-back of the game at Elland Road – the venture was a huge success as 22,000 attended. *Above*: The closed-circuit programme cover. *Below*: The programme notes explain how this opportunity for the club arose.

A piece of club history, 1968

SPECTATORS at Elland Road tonight will be taking part in a piece of club history—the first occasion on which closed circuit television has been tried out on our ground. Its subject, our Fairs Cup quarter-final with Rangers at Ibrox Stadium in Glasgow, could hardly be more enthralling.

For our fine win here over Manchester City on Saturday let us go to Glasgow at the top of the First Division, which we had reached, sliding over City by four hundredths of a goal, on Wednesday night last with our draw at Chelsea.

Rangers continued their run at the top of the Scottish First Division with a splendid 3—1 away win over Hibernian in Edinburgh. "Hibs," we may recall, were our last opponents in the Fairs Cup, and we found them a formidable side—they are still third to Rangers and Celtic in the Scottish championship.

So what you will be watching tonight is the meeting of the presently leading side in the Football League versus the presently leading side in the Scottish League—in strictly competitive football. Both Rangers and ourselves, apart from being keenly desirous of settling which is the better side, badly want to get into Europe for both the honour and the additional money that accrues from competitive European football.

Our TV contractors tonight are the well known London firm of Closed Circuit Television, Ltd., and we feel confident they will give you a good show. They have had plenty of practical experience of both indoor and outdoor sporting occasions, experience which they have brought to bear in their careful planning of tonight's "show" and its commentary.

The five screens you see are each 40 feet by 30 feet, big enough to show a good picture to even the "back row," and we have, of course, closed sections of the ground which it is technically impracticable to provide with a reasonable picture. The crowd limit tonight is indeed only 38,000 —and we had 51,818 inside last Saturday against Manchester City.

IF "HARRY" IS HERE—
Our last chairman, Mr. Harry Reynolds, made tremendous efforts during the last year or two to get closed circuit television of several of our away games, both at home and on the Continent, back to Elland Road, but always there were technical difficulties beyond solution.

However, if he is here tonight— and we trust he is either here or at Ibrox despite his continued arthritic affliction—he will be seeing his valued efforts bear fruit. One thing we cannot organise, of course, and that is the weather. We have done all we can in arranging for the kick off at Ibrox to be at 8.30 in order to allow darkness to give a better floodlit picture at Ibrox and one more clearly visible on the giant screens here.

Good viewing !

ENGLISH FOOTBALL LEAGUE
FIRST DIVISION

	HOME						AWAY						
	P	W	D	L	F	A	W	D	L	F	A	pts
LEEDS UTD.	33	14	3	0	41	11	4	6	6	15	15	45
Man. Utd.	32	12	2	3	36	14	7	5	5	27	24	45
Man. City	32	13	2	2	45	16	6	3	6	24	20	43
Liverpool	32	14	1	1	37	11	3	8	5	14	17	43
Newcastle	33	11	5	0	31	11	1	8	8	16	32	37
Everton	31	12	1	2	28	10	4	3	9	22	23	36

SCOTTISH LEAGUE
DIVISION 1

	HOME						AWAY						
	P	W	D	L	W	D	L	F	A	pts
RANGERS	27	13	2	0	11	1	0	77	23	51
Celtic	27	12	3	0	11	0	1	83	19	49
Hibernian	28	10	1	3	7	2	5	55	38	37
Dunfermline	29	9	1	5	6	4	4	56	33	35
Partick T.	29	6	4	4	6	1	8	48	58	29
Kilmarnock	28	7	4	3	4	2	8	49	50	28

Match programme cover for Rangers
v. Leeds United, 26 March 1968.

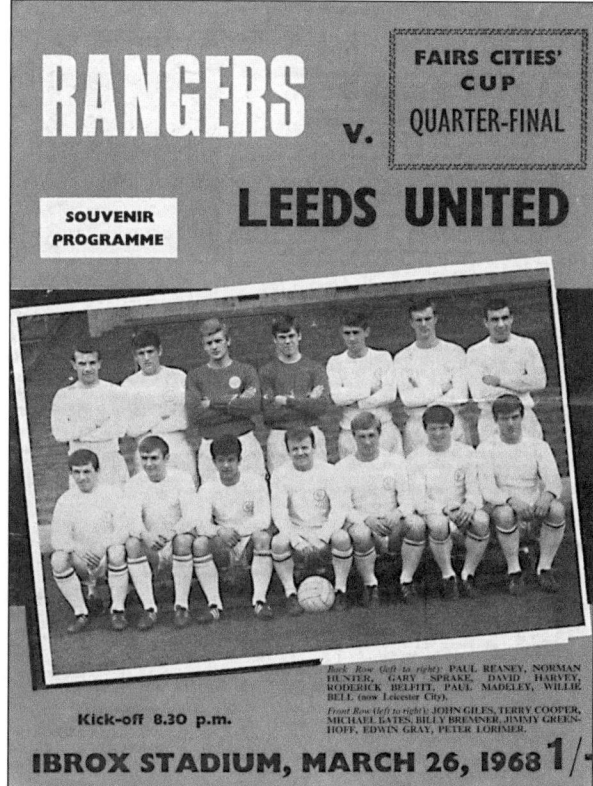

Billy Bremner and John Greig lead
out their teams before a capacity
crowd of 80,000. In a frenetic
encounter Leeds were the happier
with a goalless draw.

At Elland Road, Leeds settled the tie in the opening half when firstly Lorimer, then Giles from the penalty spot, put Leeds in control. Here, Giles clinically despatches his penalty high to Sorensen's right.

For all Rangers' effort it was Leeds who went closest to scoring again. Here, Charlton, with Madeley and Bremner in support, heads just over the bar.

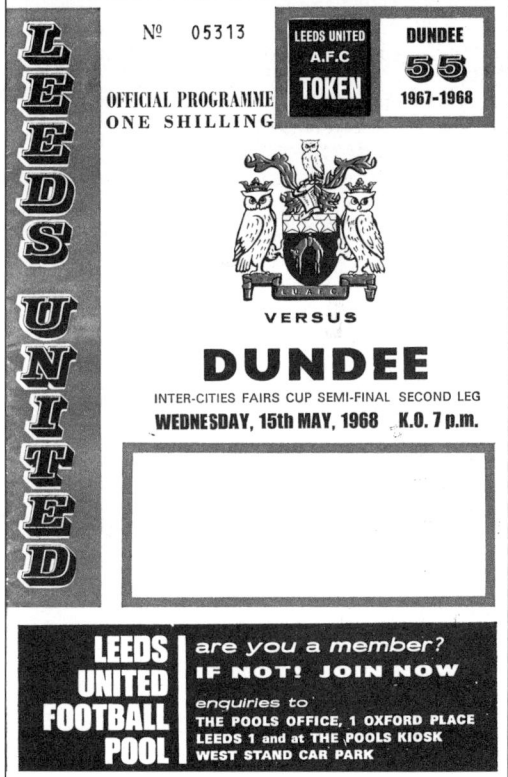

The one sour note during the game was crowd trouble, which threatened to halt the match. Here, Greig, acting on the instructions of referee Kurt Tschencher, pleads with supporters to stop throwing bottles onto the pitch.

For the third tie in succession Leeds travelled north to play Scottish opposition, this time to Dens Park and Dundee. In a tough encounter Madeley scored United's goal in a 1-1 draw. At Elland Road, a Gray strike eight minutes from time was sufficient to book Leeds a place in their second successive final. This is the programme from the second leg clash, played on 15 May 1968.

No   05313

LEEDS UNITED A.F.C
DUNDEE
55
1967-1968

OFFICIAL PROGRAMME
ONE SHILLING

TOKEN

LEEDS UNITED

VERSUS

DUNDEE

INTER-CITIES FAIRS CUP SEMI-FINAL SECOND LEG
WEDNESDAY, 15th MAY, 1968   K.O. 7 p.m.

LEEDS UNITED FOOTBALL POOL

are you a member?
IF NOT! JOIN NOW

enquiries to
THE POOLS OFFICE, 1 OXFORD PLACE
LEEDS 1 and at THE POOLS KIOSK
WEST STAND CAR PARK

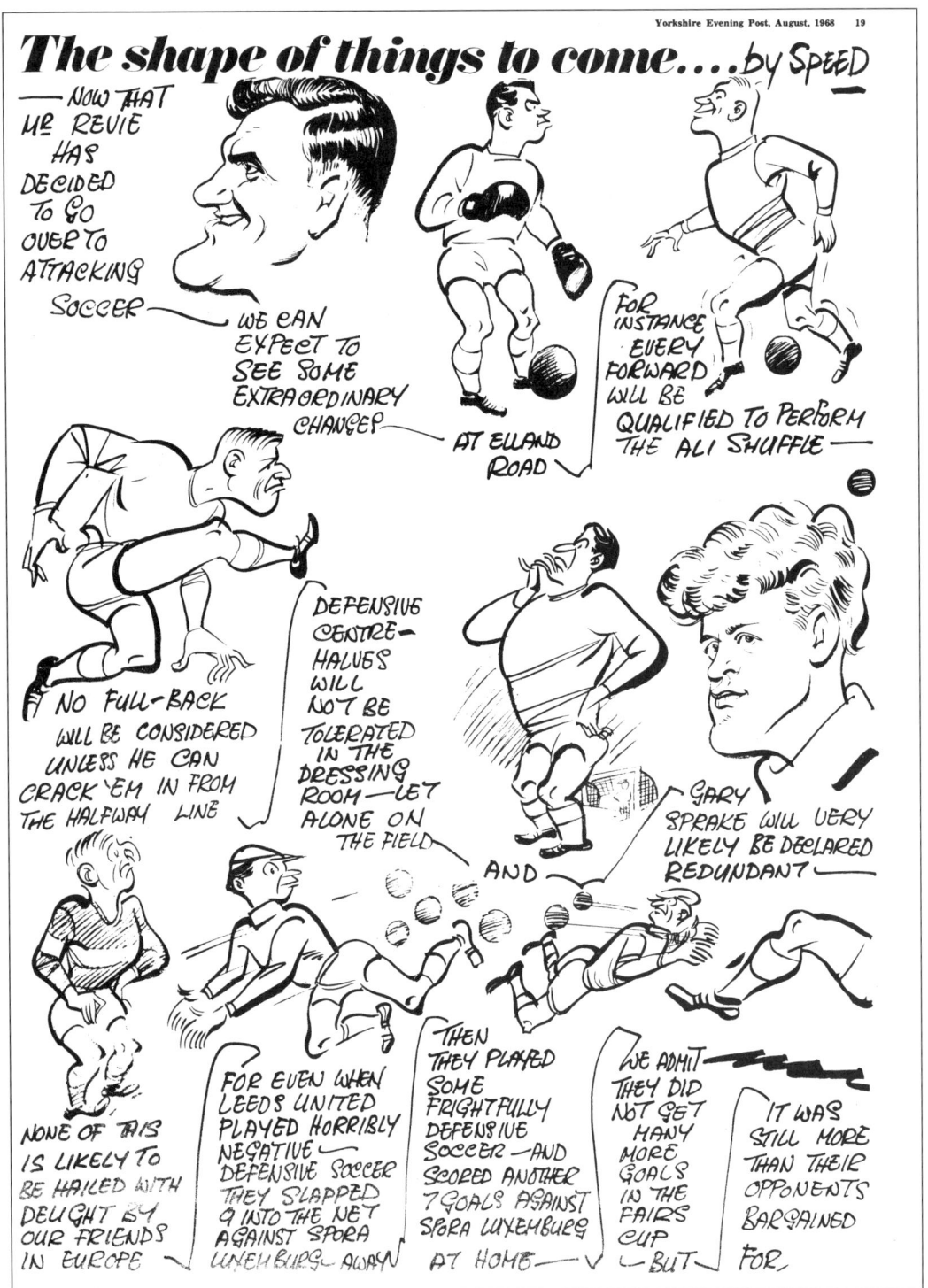

The first leg of the final against Ferencvaros at Elland Road was United's first competitive match of the 1968/69 season. Local cartoonist Speed was convinced Leeds were ready for all-comers in the new campaign.

Rowland Lindup captures the mood on the eve of the match with Ferencvaros.

Match programme cover for Leeds United
v. Ferencvaros, Fairs Cup final first leg,
7 August 1968.

Leeds battled throughout to overcome a
determined attempt by Ferencvaros to spoil
the game with rough-house tactics. The
solitary goal in the game came after forty
minutes following a Lorimer in-swinging
corner. This picture shows Jones
concentrating on the flight of the ball as
Charlton challenges Geczi.

Even though white-shirted Hungarian defenders surround him, United's number nine still manages to bundle the ball over the line.

Goalscorer Jones ends up flat on his back after making the breakthrough.

Jones' joy was short-lived. The top photograph shows Hunter complaining to the referee about Geczi's challenge that resulted in Jones being stretched off (below). After the match many pundits thought one goal would be insufficient to take to Hungary, but Revie was confident: 'It will be tough, but we have faced this type of situation before. The main thing is we kept a clean sheet, if we score one Ferencvaros have to get three.'

Match programme, Ferencvaros *v.* Leeds United, Fairs Cup final second leg, 11 September 1968.

A LEEDSI LEGÉNYEKRŐL

G. SPRAKE, a kapus már 18 éves korában szóhoz jutott a walesi válogatottban, bátor, kiváló reflexekkel rendelkező portás.

P. REANEY, a hidegfejű jobbhátvéd, aki a szélsőknek őrzése mellett a kapu előretörésben is tisztogat, segít az Angliában gyakori légi-harcban a kapusának.

J. CHARLTON 33 évével nemcsak koreinőtt, hanem a Leeds United legrégebbi „alkalmazottja" is, 15 éve áll a klub szolgálatában. A 28-szoros válogatott középhátvéd a világ egyik legjobban fejelő védője, de nemcsak saját kapujának légiterét uralja, hanem az ellenfél kapuját is veszélyezteti, ahogyan Leedsben is tette a Ferencváros elleni első döntőn. A válogatottban is négy gólt fejelt már.

T. COOPER több poszton kötött végig, mignem a balhátvéd helyén megállapodott. De nem ragaszkodik szigorúan helyéhez, gyors, előretörésre is gyakran vállalkozó labdarúgó.

N. HUNTER a „vasember", „legkeményebb angol labdardgó", a ki tudja még, hogy hány jelző kapott már a tizszeres válogatott bekötő, akinek Revie új szerepet szán az új idényben. Felfutós, a támadásokat segítő középpályásként játszatja.

B. BREMNER, a vörös, apró termetű kapitány, a csapat fáradhatatlan karmestere. Azt tartják róla, hogy sohasem fárad el, sohasem adja fel a küzdelmet. Örökmozgó, 90 percen át mindig ott tűnik fel a pályán, ahol a labda van.

J. GILES, a másik, illetve

a harmadik agrótermetű középpályás, a nagy munkabírású ír labdarúgó a Manchester Unitedből került Leedsbe.

P. LORIMER, a best-frizurás fürge csatár a hírek szerint a legnagyobb lövésű rendelkezik egész Angliában. De nem hiába skót, nem szerencsére ezekkel a lövésekkel takarékoskodott az Elland Road-stadionban.

P. MADELEY, a csapat mindenese, tulajdonléppen csatár, 8-as mezben, de védekező feladatot lát el, Revie új taktikája szerint afféle beálló játszik a 2—3—5-ös felállásban. Már válogatott is volt, Ramsey egy karadiai hivevő mérkőzésen próbálta ki. Azt mondják róla különben, hogy minden menedzser ilyen sokoldalú játékosról álmodik.

M. JONES pontosan száz-ezer fontjába került a Leeds csapatának. Már az első idény után általános a nagy-pillantás, a vétel-ár mindenegyes pennyére rászolgált.

E. GRAY Glasgowból került Leedsbe. Már a színek 23 éven alulúak válogatottjában is szóhoz jutott, Novák mellett azonban nem tudott megélni.

Cserekéret a mindörre nélyszavantők prefi múltra visszatekintő megszkovy szőke **J. GREENHOFF,** a Nottingham Forest csapatánál megvásárolt, a mölt éven Valenciában nagyszerüen játszó **R. BELFITT** és a csapat, valamint az angol liga legelső egyetlen sötétbőrű játékosa, a dél-afrikai származású **A. JOHANNESON** jöhet számításba.

A KÉT CSAPAT ÚTJA A DÖNTŐIG

A Leeds még veretlen

A Leeds csapatának tíz mérkőzését összesen 312 205 néző látta. A döntő felé vezető út mérlege: 6 győzelem, 4 döntetlen és 25:4-es gól-arány.

De menjünk sorjában.

I. forduló:
Leeds—Spora Luxemburg 9:0 (idegenben). G: Lorimer (4-et, 1-et 11-esből), Greenhoff (2), Bremner, Madeley és Jones.
Leeds—Spora Luxemburg 7:0 (otthon). G: Greenhoff (3), Cooper és Lorimer.

II. forduló:
Leeds—Partizán 2:1 (idegenben). G: Lorimer és Belfitt.
Leeds—Partizán 1:1 (otthon). G: Lorimer.

III. forduló:
Leeds—Hibernian 1:0 (otthon). G: Gray.
Leeds—Hibernian 1:1 (idegenben). G: J. Charlton.

Negyedforduló:
Leeds—Glasgow Rangers 0:0 (idegenben).
Leeds—Glasgow Rangers 2:0 (otthon). G: Lorimer és Giles (11-esből).

Idegenbeli gólnélküli döntetlen után az Elland Road-stadion 50 489 fizető nézője (ez volt a hazai VVK-beli nézőcsúcs) előtt Giles feiméggasan a jobb sarokba vágett büntetője tette fel a pontot végleg az i-re, növelte az előnyt kétgólosra.

Előddöntő:
Leeds—Dundee 1:1 (idegenben). G: Madeley.
Leeds—Dundee 1:0 (otthon). G: Gray.

Ahogy a Fradinak spanyol, úgy a Leedsnek skói csapat állta útját az elő döntői. Idegenben Madeley szerezte ki a csatásoort, az Elland Road-stadionban pedig huszonötezer néző elé szánthotte Gray góljával együtt a továbbjutást. A Leeds újra a döntőbe került. — Még egyszer nem kapunk ki a döntőben!

Idegenben remekelt a Ferencváros

A Ferencváros csapatának tíz mérkőzését jóval többen látták. Összesen 382 000 sportkedvelő volt szemtanúja a Fradi sikeres útjának.
A mérleg: 7 győzelem, 1 döntetlen és 2 vereség, a gólarány 20:11 . . .

I. forduló:
Ferencváros—Argeș Pitesti 1:3 (idegenben). G: Albert.
Ferencváros—Argeș Pitesti 4:0 (otthon). G: Albert (2), Novák (11-esből) és Varga.

Az idegenbeli csalódást keltő játék után a Népstadionban kitűnő játékra volt szükség, hogy a továbbjutásnál megérett nézősereg előtt a Fradi válogásaként kaphássónk segesetre a ránonlioná Ez volt a skói-félék előtt legzseb, legértékesebb diadala, hiszen legrővidkos csapattal, a magyar lab-

dorúgók száznál a szokatlan külülmények között, havas pályán vivták ki a jelentős győzelmet.

II. forduló:
Ferencváros—Real Zaragoza 1:2 (idegenben). G: Szőke.
Ferencváros—Real Zaragoza 3:0 (otthon). G: Novák (11-esből), Varga és Katona.

Az első mérkőzés vérbeli kupaküzdelme után a második találkozót a spanyol vendégek halni kiüavidallal téveszetették össze A Ferencváros első gólja csak nagyon nehezen, az 59. percben esett, Novák eikkor mutatta úa újna tizenegyesgyárá tudományát, de még ezután is nagyon meg kellett küzdeni a továbbjutásért. A mérkőzést különben nem az eredeti időpontban játszották le. A találkozót egyszer elcsezilék, de az értási köd miatt a 29. percben félbe-szakították. Másnap már Albert is vállalta a játékot.

III. forduló:
Ferencváros—Liverpool 1:0 (otthon). G: Katona.
Ferencváros—Liverpool 1:0 (idegenben). G: Brannikovits.

Az első mérkőzésre közvetlenül a bajnokság befejezése után, a második szamunkra szokatlan időpontban, január elején, a válogattott túrája után, a Fradi mexikói útja előtt került sor. Az első hazai mérkőzés egygólos előnye után a Liverpool tűnt esélyesebbnek, de inégis a Fradi jutott tovább. Ez volt a sédd-féléknel legzseb, legértékesebb diadala, hiszen legrövidkós csapattal, a magyar lab-

Elődöntő:
Ferencváros—Bologna 2:2 (otthon). G: Branikovits és Varga.
Ferencváros—Bologna 3:0 (idegenben). G: Varga, Havasi.

A Budapesten megszerzett minimálisnak látszó egygólos elnyt ujabb nagyszerű idegenbeli játékkal sikerült megtartani. Irában az olykor könnyelműségbőli védelem Dohonában egyszersmind ábta az olasz rohamokat. Hahavasingt a mérkőzés egyik hősének, hiszen nemcsak Hallert, az olasz egyik legjobbjáit tette hidegre, hanem még góllövésre is futotta erejéből.

On a night of unbearable tension at the Nep Stadium, Leeds withstood a barrage of attacks to clinch their first European trophy. The defence was outstanding, Sprake in particular. Time and again he came to the rescue with a series of outstanding saves, none better than one near the end from an Albert free kick. Here, he stops the Hungarian centre forward in his tracks.

A delighted Billy Bremner holds aloft the Fairs Cup after receiving it from Sir Stanley Rous. From left to right are: Reaney, Lorimer, Charlton, Bremner, Sprake, Gray, Jones, Bates.

Leeds, the first British club to win the Inter-Cities Fairs Cup, proudly show off the trophy. From left to right, back row: Norman Hunter, Mick Bates, Paul Madeley, Gary Sprake, Jack Charlton, Mike O'Grady. Front row: Terry Cooper, Billy Bremner, Paul Reaney, Mick Jones, Peter Lorimer.

United celebrate after the game in their dressing room.

The city of Leeds celebrates.

Leeds United's 1968/69 squad show off the spoils from the previous season, the Inter-Cities Fairs Cup and the Football League Cup. From left to right, back row: Paul Reaney, Jack Charlton, Paul Madeley, Mick Jones, David Harvey, Gary Sprake, Rod Belfitt, Eddie Gray, Norman Hunter. Front row: Terry Hibbitt, Johnny Giles, Terry Cooper, Billy Bremner (captain), Mike O'Grady, Mick Bates, Peter Lorimer, Albert Johanneson.

One of many souvenirs brought out to commemorate the double cup success.

A week after winning the Fairs Cup, United began their defence. This picture shows some of the players relaxing at Yeadon Airport before leaving for their first round clash in Belgium. From left to right: Harvey, Sprake, Bremner, Hunter, Charlton.

Jones' attempt at goal fails to break the deadlock against Standard Liege, with Dewalque in close attendance. The game was played on 18 September 1968 and finished 0-0.

Sprake blocks a goal-bound attempt only for the ball to rebound to Kostedde to score one of his side's goals. In an amazing second leg Liege were coasting to a comfortable 2-0 victory with forty minutes remaining. Leeds faced the ignominy of a first round defeat as defending champions. What followed demonstrated United's never-say-die attitude.

In a remarkable turnaround, Charlton gave Leeds hope with this header from a corner.

Charlton's goal ignited Leeds who tore into their opponents. The equaliser eventually arrived with this typical Lorimer-special (above), before Bremner (below) completed a sensational comeback two minutes from time to complete a 3-2 aggregate win.

United's clash with Napoli was eagerly anticipated, the Italians fielding a number of world class players including 'keeper Dino Zoff. Here is the match programme from the opening leg at Elland Road, played on 13 November 1968.

Leeds were hot! Despite having three goals disallowed, they scored twice and had other numerous opportunities. Here, Zoff denies Belfitt's close range shot.

Jack Charlton was the hero for Leeds, his immense aerial abilities outfoxing the Italian opposition. The picture above shows him heading home his second goal and the one below his celebration of it. Leeds won on the night 2-0.

As dominant as Leeds were in the first leg, the reverse was true in Italy on 27 November 1968. Napoli wiped out United's two-goal advantage and in truth deserved more. Leeds clung on desperately to the final whistle and then through extra-time. As in their tie with Bologna two seasons previously the match was decided by the toss of a disc; once again Bremner called correctly and Leeds were through. Here, a delighted Sprake, Bremner and Giles are joined by Revie.

In the third round Leeds faced Hannover 96. The first leg was one-way traffic with United easily disposing of their first German opponents. This shot shows O'Grady with the ball in the back of the net after scoring the first goal.

Leeds won the first leg 5-1 with Lorimer bagging a brace. Here, he gives Pedlasly, Hannover's 'keeper, no chance with this drive.

Jones scores United's second goal on the night after sixteen minutes in the return leg, completing a 7-2 aggregate win. The most disappointing aspect of the second game was the unnecessary dismissal of Cooper in the closing stages when his side were comfortably through to the next round. His sending off meant he would be suspended for the first leg of the quarter-final.

The first leg of the quarter-final proved to be a night of frustration for players and fans alike as Ujpest Dozsa upset the odds by defeating Leeds 1-0. Here, Fazekas celebrates Dunai's goal in the eerie silence that engulfed the ground.

For those who thought it could not get worse, it did. Here, Giles dismay is all too evident as his penalty kick is well saved by Szentmihalyi. A two-goal defeat in the return enabled Leeds to concentrate on domestic issues. Within seven weeks they were crowned First Division Champions for the first time – a place in the European Cup awaited them.

Long-playing record by SPEED

Cartoonist Speed was confident of United's prospects in the European Cup, August 1969.

Leeds United played their first tie in the European Cup on 17 September 1969 against FK Lyn Oslo. This was a side which included two drivers, two clerks, three students, a doctor, a teacher, a handball international, a full Norwegian international and Helge Ostvold, who is described in the match programme as a 'strong well-built boy'. Not surprisingly, Leeds demolished their opponents in a ten-goal humiliation of the opposition – their highest-ever victory in any form of first team football. United's scorers were O'Grady (after thirty-five seconds), Jones (three), Clarke (two), Giles (two) and Bremner (two).

Jones, standing behind summer signing Allan Clarke, watches his precision header zip into the Oslo net for one of his hat-trick. Six goals followed in the return leg, completing a 16-0 aggregate triumph and equalling United's record aggregate victory in Europe.

No 02300

LEEDS UNITED A.F.C. TOKEN

F.K. LYN OSLO
9
1969-70

OFFICIAL PROGRAMME
ONE SHILLING

LEEDS UNITED

VERSUS

EUROPEAN CUP—1st ROUND 1st LEG

F.K. LYN OSLO

WEDNESDAY, 17th SEPT., 1969   7.30 p.m.

NEXT HOME MATCHES

SATURDAY, 20th SEPTEMBER   K.O. 3.0 p.m.   F.L.
CHELSEA
WEDNESDAY, 24th SEPTEMBER   K.O. 7.30 p.m.
CHELSEA
FOOTBALL LEAGUE CUP—3rd ROUND

United faced familiar faces in the second round as Ferencvaros returned to Elland Road anxious for revenge. Leeds found this encounter with the Hungarian giants much easier than the last as they ran out comfortable 3-0 victors. Here, Lorimer whips across a perfect centre for Jones to belt in one of his two goals, Giles scoring the other.

United train at the Nep Stadium in Budapest before the second leg where they repeated the first leg result, winning 6-0 on aggregate.

They said it was the toughest draw of the European Cup quarter-finals and that Leeds would be lucky to come away with a draw, but United went out in front of 38,000 howling Standard Liege fans and defeated the home side with this Lorimer strike on 4 March 1970.

Match programme for Leeds *v.* Standard Liege, 18 March 1970.

Johnny Giles calmly sends Leeds through to the semi-finals with this penalty, the only goal of the return leg.

After defeating Liege on 4 March, United embarked on a fixture list best described as farcical. When Leeds faced Celtic in the semi-finals at Elland Road on 1 April they had played eight matches since the initial Liege win, which included the Manchester United FA Cup trilogy. In addition, this match was the end of a four-match sequence in seven days (they still had two League matches to play in the next three days!). No wonder Leeds appeared jaded and struggled to perform, going down to a solitary goal. Here, Sprake picks the ball out from the back of the net after Connolly's eighty-five-second strike.

Leeds did go close a number of times, on this occasion Clarke (hidden by Celtic's number six) just firing over.

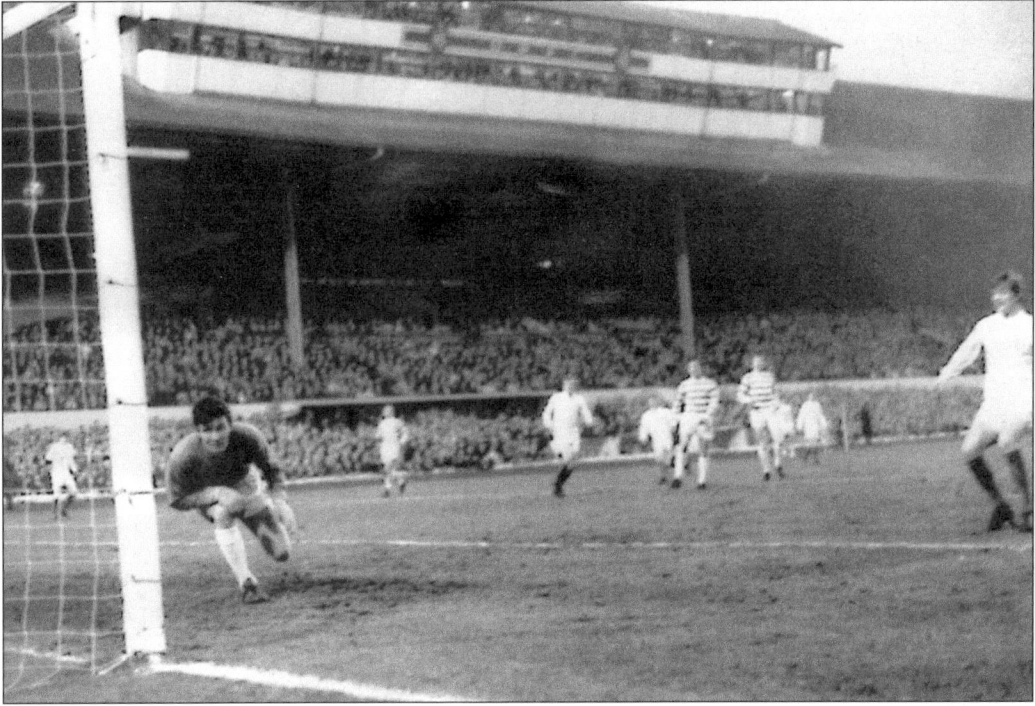

Four days after their energy-sapping FA Cup final against Chelsea, Leeds played the return with Celtic at Hampden Park in front of a record crowd of 136,000 fans. Here, Bremner crashes home an unstoppable thirty-five-yard pile driver on fourteen minutes to level the tie on aggregate.

Leeds defended desperately against wave upon wave of attacks from the green and white hoops. They kept Celtic at bay until John Hughes flicked home Bertie Auld's corner on forty-seven minutes. Hughes was also involved in the incident that changed the course of the tie when he collided with Sprake, shown here being attended to by Les Cocker before being carried off and replaced by Harvey. Harvey's first involvement was to pick the ball out of the net after a Murdoch strike made the game safe for Celtic.

A tired and dejected Billy Bremner wishes Celtic luck after United's European Cup dreams ended 3-1 on aggregate. This was a bitter end to United's European Cup campaign, where undoubtedly fatigue prevented Leeds from winning the most prestigious prize of all in club football – a title which, with a little more help from the FA over the fixture chaos, would have been well within their capabilities.

Three
Pain, Passion and Glory
1971-1974

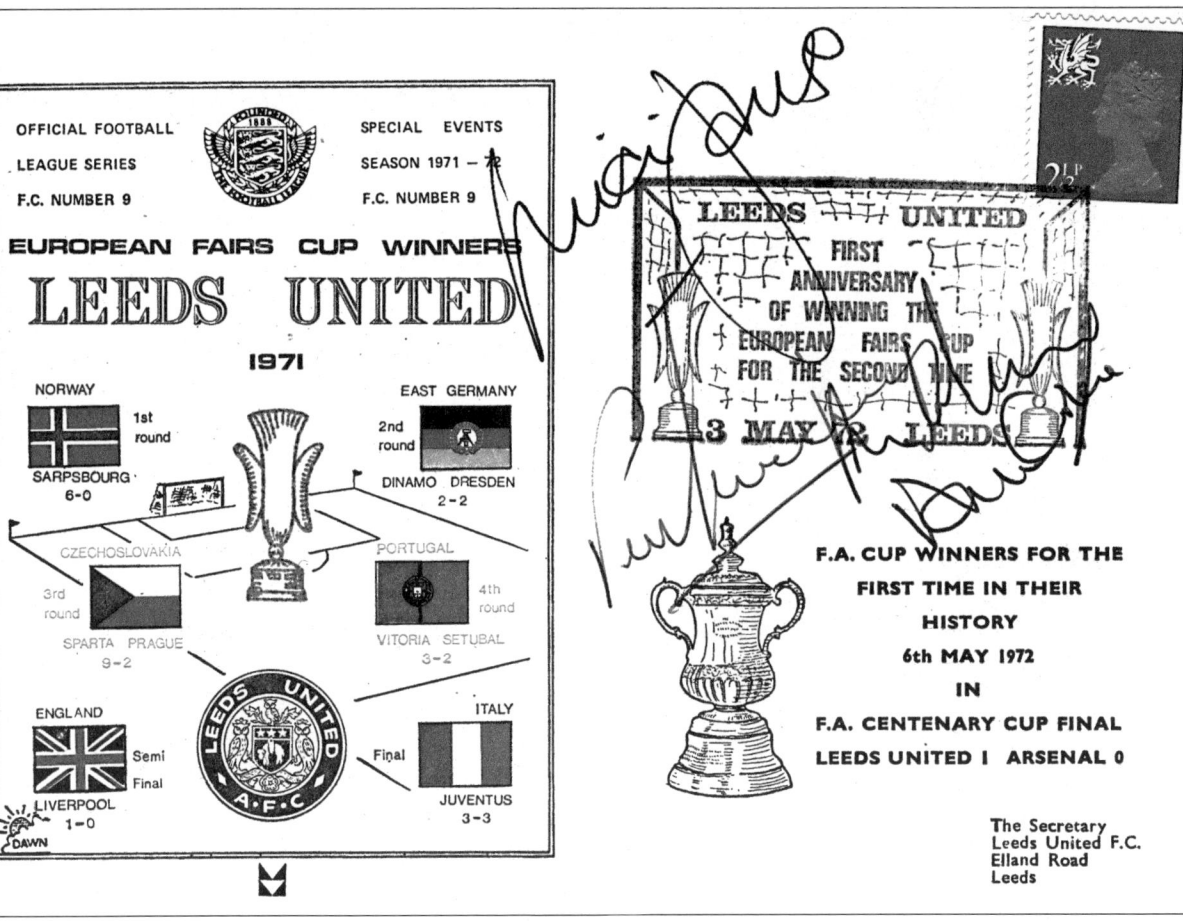

First day cover commemorating United's second Fairs Cup success.

Leeds United squad, 1970/71. From left to right, back row: Chris Galvin, Terry Yorath, David Harvey, Mick Jones, Gary Sprake, Jack Charlton, Allan Clarke, Norman Hunter, Eddie Gray, Paul Madeley. Front row: Rod Belfitt, Paul Reaney, Peter Lorimer, Johnny Giles, Billy Bremner (captain), Terry Cooper, Mick Bates, Terry Hibbitt.

For the second season running Leeds kicked off a European campaign against Norwegian opposition, but this time Sarpsborg SK made a better fight of it than their fellow countrymen did from Oslo. In the first leg a solitary Lorimer goal was all Leeds had to show from their evening's work. The return, however, was never in doubt as United ran out easy 5-0 victors.

United's second round clash was destined to be a tough affair against the East German side Dynamo Dresden. It took Leeds fifty-six minutes to find a breakthrough. In this photograph, Belfitt's header was destined for the net until Hans Dorner handled.

Lorimer nets the only goal of the tie from the resulting penalty. In a nerve-racking return leg Leeds were edged out 2-1, but qualified for the next round on the away goals rule for the first time.

WEST STAND PADDOCK

EUROPEAN FAIRS CUP

THIRD ROUND FIRST LEG

LEEDS UNITED

versus

CKD SPARTA PRAGUE

ELLAND ROAD, LEEDS

Wednesday, 2nd Dec., 1970

Kick-off 7.30 p.m.

RESERVED SEAT

Admit through Turnstile as allocated

ROW   SEAT No.

GG   85

ADMISSION £1·00 (20/-)

Holder to retain this portion for
inspection if necessary.

L. M. LEE (Printers) Ltd., 105/106a North St., Leeds 7

Vintage Leeds! Goals from Clarke (above), Bremner, Charlton and Gray (two) all before half-time blew away their third round Czechoslovakian opponents Sparta Prague. An exceptional performance, they went on to win the match 6-0. In Prague, Leeds carried on in a similar vein, scoring three times without reply in the first half, the tie ending 3-2 (9-2 on aggregate).

LEEDS UNITED		CF. VITORIA
WHITE SHIRTS WHITE SHORTS	Referee : Mr. MAENNIG East Germany	SETUBAL GREEN AND WHITE STRIPED SHIRTS GREEN SHORTS AND SOCKS
1. HARVEY, David		1. TORRES, Joaquim
2. DAVEY, Nigel		2. REBELO, Francis
3. REANEY, Paul		3. CARRICO, Manuel
4. BATES, Mick		4. WAGNER, Pereira
5. CHARLTON, Jack	**BROWN WHITE** Ford **MAIN DEALER**	5. CARDOSO, Carlos
6. HUNTER, Norman		6. MENDES, José
7. LORIMER, Peter		7. GUERREIRO, Felix
8. BELFITT, Rod		8. MARIA, José
9. JONES, Mick		9. BATISTA, Vitor
10. GILES, Johnny	Linesmen :	10. OCTAVIO, Machado
11. MADELEY, Paul	Mr. EINBECK East Germany (Red Flag)	11. JOAO, Jacinto
Sub...............		Sub...............
Sub...............	Mr. SHULTZ East Germany (Yellow Flag)	Sub...............
Sub...............		Sub...............
Sub...............		Sub...............
Sub...............	Any alteration to these teams will be announced over the loudspeakers.	Sub...............

The quarter-final draw had a strong English presence with Fairs Cup holders Arsenal taking on FC Cologne, Liverpool facing Bayern Munich and Leeds drawing the crack Portugese outfit, CF Vitoria Setubal. This is the team sheet from the home leg, played on 10 March 1971.

Leeds recovered from conceding a goal in ninety seconds to win the first leg 2-1, Lorimer blasting home the equaliser with this thunderous shot. With a quarter of an hour remaining, Leeds were awarded a hotly disputed penalty for handball, which Giles calmly dispatched. Setubal's players reactions in surrounding the referee *en masse* to protest the award were so ugly that Phil Brown, then sports editor of the *Yorkshire Evening Post,* was moved to suggest that he wouldn't be surprised if Setubal had the return leg transferred to the nearest bull ring. In a frantic second leg that finished 1-1, Lorimer's strike was sufficient to take Leeds through to the semi-finals for the fourth time in five attempts.

Leeds faced a familiar trip in the semi-finals when they were drawn to play Liverpool, with the first leg at Anfield on 14 April 1971. In a typical blood-and-thunder encounter between the top two teams in England, a crucial header on sixty-seven minutes from Bremner gave United a first-leg victory. Here, the referee points to the centre circle after Bremner's effort.

Bremner celebrates with Charlton after his goal. After the match Bremner, returning to play as a make-shift centre forward in only his second game of 1971, said of his goal: 'It was a great feeling seeing the ball go in, and especially in front of the Kop. I'm tired and it was a big thing for me to come back in a match of this importance.'

The second leg was disappointing as a spectacle, but tense nevertheless. The best of the chances in this goalless encounter fell to Jones, who headed against the bar, and Heighway, who forced Sprake into a fingertip save. Before the hour Revie's attacking options were severely weakened as he was forced to replace Clarke and Jones, through injury, with Reaney and Jordan. With Jordan playing as the solitary front man, United packed the midfield and succeeded in smothering Liverpool's attacks. Leeds were through to the final once again.

Against Juventus in the final, Leeds faced the best. To win the trophy United would have to overcome a team valued at £2,000,000, which included such legends as Causio, Bettaga, Anastasi, Capello and the German, Helmut Haller. Here, the captains shake hands before the first leg on 26 May 1971.

On the pitch Giles and Capello struggle to kick the ball forward as the match descends into farce.

Both benches shelter from the torrential rain. The referee eventually had no alternative but to abandon the game after fifty-six minutes.

Speed captures the waterlog incident in his weekly cartoon.

The rematch two days later saw Leeds reshuffle their side, with Madeley replacing the unfortunate Eddie Gray (dislocated shoulder) in midfield and Reaney returning in defence. The match was an exciting encounter with Leeds twice coming from behind to record a magnificent 2-2 draw. In the early exchanges Leeds settled the better. Here, Jones pressurises goalkeeper Piloni and Salvadore.

Juventus took the lead a little against the run of play after twenty-seven minutes with a flowing move. Haller, dispossessing Cooper, moved the ball on through Anastasi to Causio. His cross found Bettaga who slammed home an unstoppable shot. Early in the second half Leeds equalised through Madeley's (above, out of shot) speculative twenty-five-yard drive which deflected off Salvadore, wrong-footing Piloni.

After fifty-five minutes, Juventus regained the lead when Capello hit a rising shot through a packed defence into the top corner of the net. With quarter of an hour remaining Tancredi misjudged Cooper's cross and Bates (above), on for the injured Jones, volleyed home with his first touch. After the match a proud Revie said, 'This was one of our best ever displays in European football. It was not so much the result but the performance that pleased me. We were world class.'

The team sheet for the replay shows just how many world-class players were on display from both sides.

THE TEAMS

LEEDS UNITED WHITE SHIRTS WHITE SHORTS	F.C. JUVENTUS BLACK AND WHITE VERTICAL STRIPED SHIRTS WHITE SHORTS AND SOCKS
1. Gary Sprake	1. Piloni
2. Paul Reaney	2. Luciana Spinosi
3. Terry Cooper	3. Gian Marchetti
4. Billy Bremner	4. Giuseppe Furino
5. Jack Charlton	5. Francesco Morini
6. Norman Hunter	6. S. Salvadore
7. Peter Lorimer	7. Helmut Haller
8. Alan Clarke	8. Franco Causio
9. Mick Jones	9. Pietro Anastasi
10. Johnny Giles	10. Fabio Capello
11. Eddie Gray	11. Roberto Bettega
12. Paul Madeley	
Sub.	Sub.
Sub.	Sub.
Sub.	Sub.
Sub.	Sub.
Sub.	Sub.

ANY ALTERATION TO THESE TEAMS
WILL BE ANNOUNCED OVER THE LOUDSPEAKERS

REFEREE :
Herr Glöckner
LEIPZIG, EAST GERMANY

LINESMAN : **Herr Riedel** East Germany (Red Flag)	LINESMAN : **Herr Kunze** East Germany (Yellow Flag)

Chairman's Message

On behalf of the Directors, Officials, Players and Supporters of Leeds United Football Club, I extend a hearty welcome to the Directors and Officials of Juventus Football Club.

Our visitors are one of the greatest Club sides in the world, and their brand of football has earned acclaim wherever the game is played.

It is a great tribute to Leeds that Juventus are turning out their full league team, and I would like to thank the Directors of Juventus for their kindness and co-operation.

I would also thank our supporters for their attendance this evening, and hope they will see a game of football to be remembered.

P. A. Woodward

Chairman.

The Path to the Final
HOW THEY GOT THERE

LEEDS UNITED

FIRST ROUND
Sarpsborg (Norway) away 1—0 Lorimer.
Sarpsborg home 5—0
Charlton 2, Bremner 2, Lorimer.
SECOND ROUND
Dinamo Dresden (E. Germany) home 1—0
Lorimer (penalty).
Dinamo Dresden away 1—2* Jones.
*Leeds won tie on away goals.
THIRD ROUND
Sparta Prague (Czech.) home 6—0
Clarke, Chovanec (o.g.), Bremner, Gray 2, Charlton.
Sparta Prague away 3—2
Gray, Clarke, Belfitt.
QUARTER FINAL
V. Setubal (Portugal) home 2—1
Lorimer, Giles (penalty).
Vitoria Setubal away 1—1 Lorimer.
SEMI-FINAL
Liverpool away 1—0 Bremner.
Liverpool home 0—0

FINAL (First Leg) — F.C. JUVENTUS
FINAL (Second Leg) — LEEDS UNITED

page two

F.C. JUVENTUS

FIRST ROUND
Rumelange (Luxem.) home 7—0
Rumelange away 4—0
Juventus won 11—0 on aggregate.
SECOND ROUND
Barcelona (Spain) away 2—1
Barcelona home 2—1
Juventus won 4—2 on aggregate.
THIRD ROUND
Pecsi Dozsa (Hungary) away 1—0
Pecsi Dozsa home 2—0
Juventus won 3—0 on aggregate.
QUARTER FINAL
F.C. Twente Enschede (Holland) home 2—0
F.C. Twente Enschede away 2—2
(After extra time)
Juventus won on aggregate 4—2.
SEMI-FINAL
F.C. Cologne (W. Germany) away 1—1
Begetta
F.C. Cologne home 2—0 Capello, Anastasi.
Juventus won 3—1 on aggregate.

| LEEDS UNITED | At Turin |
| F.C. JUVENTUS | At Elland Road |

In the match programme United's chairman Percy Woodward welcomes Juventus in his notes.

The return at Elland Road on 2 June 1971 was equally as exciting as the first encounter. Here, Allan Clarke gives Leeds the lead after twelve minutes.

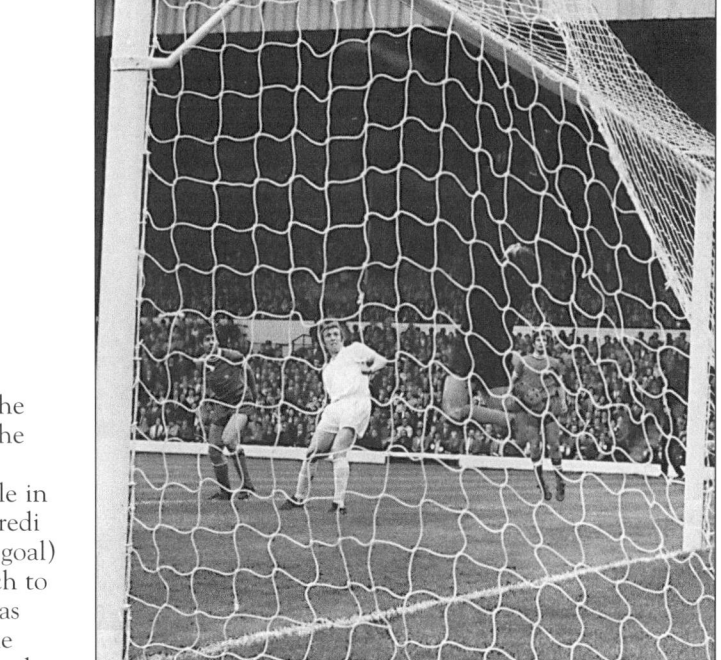

United's lead didn't last long as, just seven minutes later, Anastasi capitalised on a rare defensive mix-up to slot the ball past an advancing Sprake for the equaliser.

With chances at both ends the result was in doubt right to the end, indeed Leeds fans were screaming for the final whistle in the dying stages. Here, Tancredi (on for the injured Piloni in goal) pulls off the save of the match to deny Jones. The 1-1 result was sufficient for Leeds to win the Fairs Cup on the away-goals rule.

Bremner receives the Fairs Cup for the second time.

The trophy is raised to the Kop during the lap of honour. Joining Bremner are, from left to right: Cooper, Charlton, Hunter, Giles.

Leeds celebrate in their dressing room after the match. From left to right, back row: Jack Charlton, Norman Hunter, Gary Sprake, Billy Bremner, Johnny Giles, Peter Lorimer, Mick Bates, Les Cocker, Allan Clarke, Paul Madeley. Front row: Bob English, Eddie Gray, Terry Yorath, Paul Reaney, Mick Jones, Terry Cooper, Rod Belfitt, Terry Hibbit, Don Revie.

Leeds United squad, 1971/72. From left to right, back row: Rod Belfitt, Norman Hunter, Gary Sprake, David Harvey, Joe Jordan, Terry Yorath. Middle row: John Faulkner, Chris Galvin, Mick Jones, Paul Madeley, Allan Clarke, Jack Charlton. Front row: Paul Reaney, Mick Bates, Peter Lorimer, Johnny Giles, Billy Bremner (captain), Nigel Davey, Terry Cooper. As the last winners of the trophy, Leeds travelled to Barcelona, the first winners, to determine the final destiny of the Fairs Cup. When the match was played on 22 September 1971 it was United's twelfth game in thirty-nine days of the new season and it showed, the Catalonians comfortably winning 2-1 over a lacklustre Leeds. The only bright note was nineteen-year-old Joe Jordan's first goal for the club. The UEFA Cup replaced the Fairs Cup and Leeds' first opponents, Lierse SK, could only be rated as mediocre. The two legs were played either side of the play-off match with Barcelona. Although several key players were missing for the ties, Leeds still managed a 2-0 away victory, but somehow failed to hold on to their comfortable advantage in the return. The result, a 4-0 humiliation, left the sparse crowd of 18,700 stunned as they watched what is surely the club's worst-ever European display. To date this result is the club's only first round exit in a European competition.

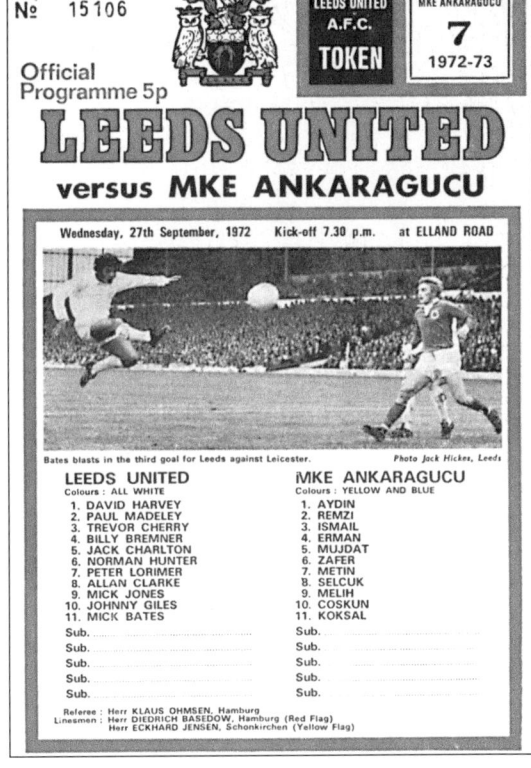

In 1972/73 United played in the Cup Winners' Cup for the first time as FA Cup holders. The first round draw was unkind as Leeds were despatched to play in the hostile atmosphere of Ankara, Turkey. It came as no surprise that Ankaragucu scored from a debatable penalty in a tie that finished 1-1, Jordan scoring for Leeds. However, United overcome their Turkish opponents in the second leg with this powerful Jones header.

Nº 15106

LEEDS UNITED
A.F.C.
TOKEN

MKE ANKARAGUCU
7
1972-73

Official
Programme 5p

LEEDS UNITED
versus MKE ANKARAGUCU

Wednesday, 27th September, 1972   Kick-off 7.30 p.m.   at ELLAND ROAD

Bates blasts in the third goal for Leeds against Leicester.   *Photo Jack Hickes, Leeds*

LEEDS UNITED
Colours : ALL WHITE

1. DAVID HARVEY
2. PAUL MADELEY
3. TREVOR CHERRY
4. BILLY BREMNER
5. JACK CHARLTON
6. NORMAN HUNTER
7. PETER LORIMER
8. ALLAN CLARKE
9. MICK JONES
10. JOHNNY GILES
11. MICK BATES

Sub.
Sub.
Sub.
Sub.
Sub.

MKE ANKARAGUCU
Colours : YELLOW AND BLUE

1. AYDIN
2. REMZI
3. ISMAIL
4. ERMAN
5. MUJDAT
6. ZAFER
7. METIN
8. SELCUK
9. MELIH
10. COSKUN
11. KOKSAL

Sub.
Sub.
Sub.
Sub.
Sub.

Referee : Herr KLAUS OHMSEN, Hamburg
Linesmen : Herr DIEDRICH BASEDOW, Hamburg (Red Flag)
Herr ECKHARD JENSEN, Schonkirchen (Yellow Flag)

The match programme from the return leg with Ankaragucu.

United faced another awful journey in the next round, travelling to East German side Carl Zeiss Jena. After a dour first leg, which ended goalless, Leeds appeared grateful to be home. Here, Eddie Gray and Billy Bremner enter the main hall at Yeadon Airport.

In the return game Leeds dominated, time and again being denied. Eventually pre-season signing Trevor Cherry broke the deadlock before this Jones header saw United home 2-0.

Against Rapid Bucharest in the quarter-finals, a 5-0 home victory in the first leg settled the tie: Giles, Clarke, Lorimer (two) and Jordan scoring. Whether this was enough to entice Leeds fans to spend hard-earned cash on this 'once-in-a-lifetime' exclusive offer is unclear, but whoever did make the trek witnessed a comfortable 3-1 triumph in conditions more suited to the Arctic Circle (below).

Leeds traditionally had difficulties overcoming Yugoslavian opposition, therefore when the semi-finals paired them with Hajduk Split they anticipated and received a testing examination of their ability. In the first leg at Elland Road Clarke proved to be the hero, scoring the only goal of the match on 11 September 1973.

Unfortunately, the hero soon became the villain. Here, Clarke walks disconsolately from the field after being sent off – no doubt contemplating his misfortune at missing out on the return and a possible final. In Split, Leeds, though victorious on aggregate after their goalless draw, suffered another blow to their final aspirations as a booking for Bremner meant the skipper would also miss out.

Leeds United *v.* AC Milan, European Cup Winners' Cup final, 16 May 1973. AC Milan scored after just four minutes, but in truth the match was reduced to farce by an outrageous display of officiating by local referee Christos Mikhas, whose bias towards the Italians bordered on the obscene. Time and again he denied Leeds free kicks and in particular three blatant penalties – Mikhas may as well have been wearing an AC Milan shirt. United never stood a chance. Their patience eventually ran out with Hunter being sent off for retaliation, following one horrendous challenge too many. The Greek fans demonstrated their disapproval after Milan's 1-0 triumph at the presentation by giving a champion-like reception to a distraught United, whilst showing nothing but hostility to the victors.

The outstretched arms of David Harvey fail to prevent this deflected free kick finding the net for AC Milan's winner. United's side was: David Harvey, Paul Reaney, Trevor Cherry, Mick Bates, Terry Yorath, Norman Hunter, Peter Lorimer, Joe Jordan, Mick Jones, Frank Gray (Gordon McQueen), Paul Madeley.

Leeds United squad, 1973/74. From left to right, back row: Peter Lorimer, Eddie Gray, Mick Bates, Allan Clarke, Norman Hunter, Gordon McQueen, Roy Ellam, Paul Reaney, Frank Gray. Front row: Terry Yorath, Gary Sprake, Trevor Cherry, Joe Jordan, Johnny Giles, David Harvey, Paul Madeley, Billy Bremner (captain), Mick Jones.

eurosoccer

euroleague

	P	W	D	L	F	A	Pts.
Leeds United	74	40	21	13	134	53	101
Rangers	82	41	12	29	145	121	94
Celtic	61	38	10	13	128	48	86
Manchester United	57	36	11	10	129	56	83
Liverpool	64	34	14	16	110	48	82
Tottenham	44	29	5	10	115	48	63
Hibernian	49	25	7	17	96	75	57
Dunfermline	35	19	5	11	67	36	43
Chelsea	30	16	9	5	63	25	41
Arsenal	30	16	5	9	59	23	37
Cardiff	32	13	11	8	53	30	37
Dundee	29	17	2	10	55	40	36
Newcastle United	24	13	6	5	37	21	32
Wolves	24	11	6	7	45	32	28
Manchester City	22	11	4	7	36	19	26

Forget the Liverpools, Celtics and Rangers of the soccer world . . . your very own Leeds United would be flying high at the top if ever a European table was produced. Going on the records of all the successful British clubs in Europe in the last few years, United's record is second to none. If a points system was used like the one which operates in The Football League—two for a win, one for a draw—United would be seven points clear at the top from nearest challengers Rangers.

So, we've got out that table for you—and we're looking closely at United's record as they prepare for tonight's second leg of the first round of this season's U.E.F.A. Cup. United have played 74 matches in European competitions of all designations which have brought them no less than 40 wins, 21 draws and just a tiny 13 defeats. They've scored 134 goals, which is only bettered by Rangers, but have conceded just 53, against Rangers 121.

To be fair to Rangers however, they've played more European games than any other British side (82) and not surprisingly have scored more goals than anyone else. United are now under way in their ninth season

on the trot in Europe. They've two trophies to show for it, the Fairs Cup (now the U.E.F.A. Cup) in 1968 and 1971 and hold a British club record for appearing in finals—the Fairs Cup in 1966-67 and last season's Cup Winners' Cup in Salonika.

"People in Leeds have come to expect that we automatically play in Europe season in and season out . . . but they must remember that is an honour and an achievement to qualify," says United manager Don Revie who is a firm believer in the importance of European football.

"Think what an honour it would be for the fans at Stoke or Birmingham to have their side in Europe just once, let alone nine years running. Ipswich fans too are overjoyed at seeing their side take on Europe's best this season."

He adds: "We must go on chasing everything despite what people may say about too many competitions spoiling our chances of winning even one. We are fully hoping for another good run in Europe because quite honestly, we need the money it brings to keep on re-developing Elland Road in the way we have set our minds on."

UEFA CUP

Aberdeen 4, Finn Harps 1
    Attendance : 10,700
Dundee 1, Twente Enschde 3
    Attendance : 13,000
Hibernian 2, IBK Keflavik 0
    Attendance : 13,652
Ipswich Town 1, Real Madrid 0
    Attendance : 25,064
Stromsgodset 1, Leeds United 1
    Attendance : 16,276
Standard Liege 6, Ards 1
Grasshoppers Zurich 1, Tottenham 5

Eskisehirapor (Turkey) 0,
  F.C. Colgne 0
Panathinaikos 1, D.F.K. Belgrade 2
Tatran Presov (Czechoslovakia) 4,
  Valez Nostar (Yugaslavia) 2
Dynamo Tbilisi (U.S.S.R.) 4,
  Slavia Sofia 1
V.S.S. Kosice (Czech.) 1, Honved 0
Carl Zeiss Jena (G.D.R.) 3,
  Mikkelin Pallollijat (Finland) 0
Ferencvaros 0, Gwardia Warsaw 1
B.K. 1903 Copenhagen 2,
  A.I.K. Stockholm 1
Feneribahcce 5, Arges Pitesti 0
Fredrikstad 0, Dynamo Kiev 1
Ruch Chorzow 4,
  Wuppertal (W. Germany) 1
Admira Wacker (Austria) 1,
  Inter-Milan 0

Second Leg
V.F.B. Stuttgart 4,
  Olympiakos Nicosia 0
Stuttgart win 13—0 on aggregate.

As United embarked on another UEFA Cup campaign, statisticians produced this league table that identified Leeds as the most successful British side in European competition. Whilst there was no single factor for this accolade, there is no doubt that their achievement was down to consistency, resilience and a never-say-die attitude. In the first round Leeds once again faced Norwegian opponents and, for all 'anoraks' out there who are interested, their opponents, Stromsgodset Idrettsforening, are the team with the longest name the club have ever faced. After the first leg ended in a 1-1 draw, with Clarke scoring United's goal, Stromsgodset became yet another team to be hammered at Elland Road in the return.

Allan Clarke scores United's first against Stromsgodset in a 6-1 rout, 3 October 1973.

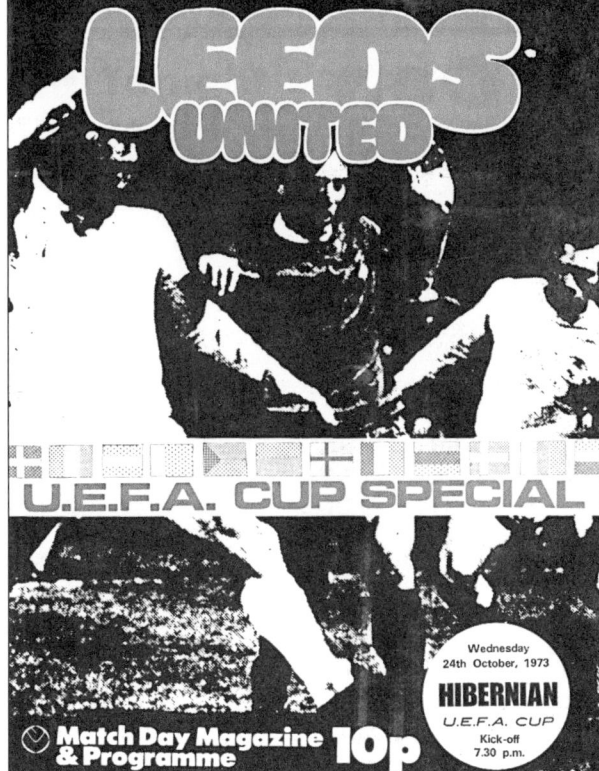

Leeds faced Hibernian in the next round, the Scots achieving a creditable goalless draw at Elland Road in the first leg.

the hibernian job

WERE THEY RIGHT TO PROTEST?

Just a few minutes after ten o'clock on a clear fresh night in Edinburgh exactly three weeks ago tonight, Billy Bremner calmly placed the ball down on the penalty spot, took a few paces back then cheekily lashed his shot high into the net. As United's skipper reeled away, arms held high in victory, his actions were reflected by a small group standing in the centre circle at Hibernian's Easter Road. One of that group was Don Revie.

Was he wrong to be there? Did he coach United's five penalty kickers out there on the pitch? Did he commit an offence? Incredibly enough, these were the questions being asked in Hibernian's boardroom at a hastily convened directors' meeting within minutes of the match ending. And soon after that, the wires were buzzing between Edinburgh and Berne as Hibernian cabled an official protest under the section of UEFA rules dealing with penalty taking to decide UEFA Cup ties.

The result of all this was learned a week ago in a cryptic telegram from UEFA. "The Control and Disciplinary Committee . . . dealt with the protest lodged by Hibernian FC. Having examined the official reports and the protest of Hibernian FC the Committee decides:

. . . to suspend Mr. D. Revie *(Manager of Leeds FC)* for one match in the UEFA Club Competitions for having entered the field of play and for having spoken to some players in the vicinity of the touchline during the taking of kicks from the penalty spot. Mr. Revie will therefore not be permitted to act in any official capacity on the occasion of the next match. He will not be permitted to enter the dressing room of the team nor to approach the field of play. He may attend the match solely in the capacity of a spectator.

. . . to censure Mr. L. Cocker *(Coach of Leeds United FC)* for having entered the field of play without the referee's permission on the same occasion . . .

. . . to reject the protest of Hibernian FC. The behaviour of Mr. Revie and Mr. Cocker . . . has had no decisive influence as to the regularity of the taking of*

the said kicks from the penalty spot."

So, on what must be one of the longest drawn out 'matches' ever, United did eventually win. But why did Hibernian seek to have United ruled out on what was, at best, a minute technicality? Is it fair to say that after Hibs' fighting 0—0 draw at Elland Road in the first leg of the tie, passions were running high North of the Border about the outcome of the second leg. Seldom can a team have taken the field so utterly convinced that its opponents did not have a chance as Hibs that night three weeks ago.

From the Scottish Press had come stories headlined "Revie insults Scotland" and others to that effect when United's injury and illness decimated squad was announced. True, there was no Norman Hunter, no David Harvey, no Mick Jones, no Johnny Giles, no Gordon McQueen. But the side that lined up at Easter Road still contained no less than five international stars—and any team would be proud of that.

Hibernian had been lulled into believing that United were 'pushovers'. Yet, nothing was further from the truth. It was Don Revie who said after the match that never had he seen "such a magnificent performance from any side over two hours" as his United that night. So the Hibs' protest was probably born out of frustration as much as anything else.

But did they really have a case. The UEFA rules governing the taking of penalty kicks might be construed as being a little vague. Sections five and nine of Article 11 state the following . . .

"Only the players who are on the field of play at the end of the match, i.e. at the end of extra-time, shall be eligible to take part in the penalty kicking.

All players, other than the two goalkeepers and the player taking the kick, shall remain in

the centre circle whilst the taking of the penalty kicks is in progress."

No mention of the entitlement of managers to be there, no mention of whether trainers can or cannot go on the pitch.

At the end of extra time, both Don Revie and Eddie Turnbull, the Hibs' manager, went on to the field while the referee tossed a coin to decide the end at which the penalties were to be taken. When Hibs' skipper Pat Stanton faced up to 17 year old Glan Letheran with the first kick, Don Revie was standing in the centre circle together with United's takers—and together with Eddie Turnbull and one of the linesmen. As Stanton hit his kick against a post, Eddie Turnbull left the field. All Don Revie was seen to do was to hold the track suit jackets of each United player as he strode forward to take a penalty. Was this coaching?

During this time, the other players, of both sides, were on the edge of the pitch in front of the trainer's dug-outs and Les Cocker was on the field. But then so was Hibs' trainer for a time. And both sets of players were 'guilty' of leaving the pitch for soft drinks. So who was guilty, who was innocent and was there a charge to answer?

It has always been a principle of British law that any accused man has the right to state his case. United were not afforded this opportunity. But UEFA came down on United's side so why should the matter be resurrected again? Simply that, ostensibly, UEFA collected evidence not only from the referee and their official observer but also from Hibernian. There is no harm in that—Hibs, as protesters, had to state their case. But, United were not given the chance of reply.

It poses a succinct question. What would have been the feeling at Elland Road if UEFA had come down on Hibs' side? But this slight breeze in a very small teacup is now over and tonight United give living proof of being in the third round. Controversy or not, Leeds United march on successive season of Continental competition. It would appear that the UEFA Committee members have the right attitude—results should be won on the field not as a result of lobbying in the corridors of power.

In the League, United were flying, but clearly European success was not Revie's top priority as he rested a number of players from both ties. Leeds received incredible criticism from the Scottish press. Headlines suggested United were insulting Scottish football by their team selections and that they were demeaning the competition itself. Even so, a weakened Leeds still produced a magnificent performance at Easter Road with Bremner starring in a sweeper role. The match finished 0-0 after 120 minutes, taking United into their first-ever penalty shoot-out, which they won 5-4. Controversy still raged at the end as Hibernian officials immediately protested at Revie's presence in the semi-circle during the shoot-out, a clear breach of Article 11 of UEFA's rules. The result from their protest was that, although the result stood, Revie was suspended for one match from entering his team's dressing room and the field of play.

Two seasons after Vitoria Setubal had felt robbed by Leeds, the Portugese side gained their revenge. In front of their smallest-ever European home crowd, a paltry 14,196, United shaded a tight encounter thanks to a solitary Cherry goal. In the return Setubal's fast flowing football was far too strong for a much-weakened Leeds side, Gary Liddell scoring United's goal in their 3-1 defeat. This would be Don Revie's last match in charge of Leeds in Europe, as he would take on the challenge of managing England at the end of the season, but not before guiding Leeds to a second League title and another tilt at the European Cup.

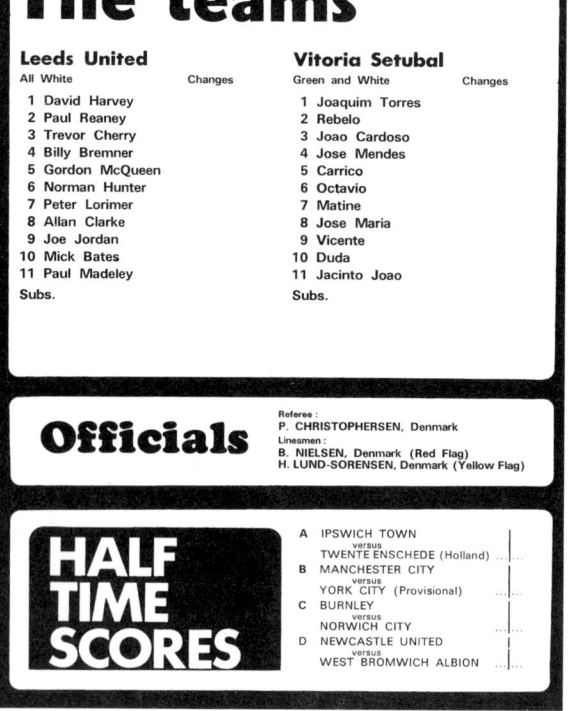

The teams

Leeds United		Vitoria Setubal	
All White	Changes	Green and White	Changes
1 David Harvey		1 Joaquim Torres	
2 Paul Reaney		2 Rebelo	
3 Trevor Cherry		3 Joao Cardoso	
4 Billy Bremner		4 Jose Mendes	
5 Gordon McQueen		5 Carrico	
6 Norman Hunter		6 Octavio	
7 Peter Lorimer		7 Matine	
8 Allan Clarke		8 Jose Maria	
9 Joe Jordan		9 Vicente	
10 Mick Bates		10 Duda	
11 Paul Madeley		11 Jacinto Joao	
Subs.		Subs.	

Officials

Referee
P. CHRISTOPHERSEN, Denmark
Linesmen
B. NIELSEN, Denmark (Red Flag)
H. LUND-SORENSEN, Denmark (Yellow Flag)

HALF TIME SCORES

A	IPSWICH TOWN	
	versus	
	TWENTE ENSCHEDE (Holland)	
B	MANCHESTER CITY	
	versus	
	YORK CITY (Provisional)	
C	BURNLEY	
	versus	
	NORWICH CITY	
D	NEWCASTLE UNITED	
	versus	
	WEST BROMWICH ALBION	

Four
Life After Don
1975-1979

Souvenir pennant celebrating United's achievement in reaching the European Cup final, 28 May 1975.

United were a club in turmoil when they embarked on their second European Cup campaign. After Revie's departure and Brian Clough's shambolic forty-four-day tenure, United's first round match was played whilst the team was under the temporary control of caretaker manager Maurice Lindley. It didn't appear to have any adverse effect on the players as FC Zurich were defeated 4-1 in the opening leg at Elland Road. Here, Clarke scores one of his brace of goals from a narrow angle.

Lorimer crashes home a penalty in United's win over Zurich. The three-goal margin of victory was more than sufficient to take Leeds through to the next round, despite a 2-1 defeat in Switzerland.

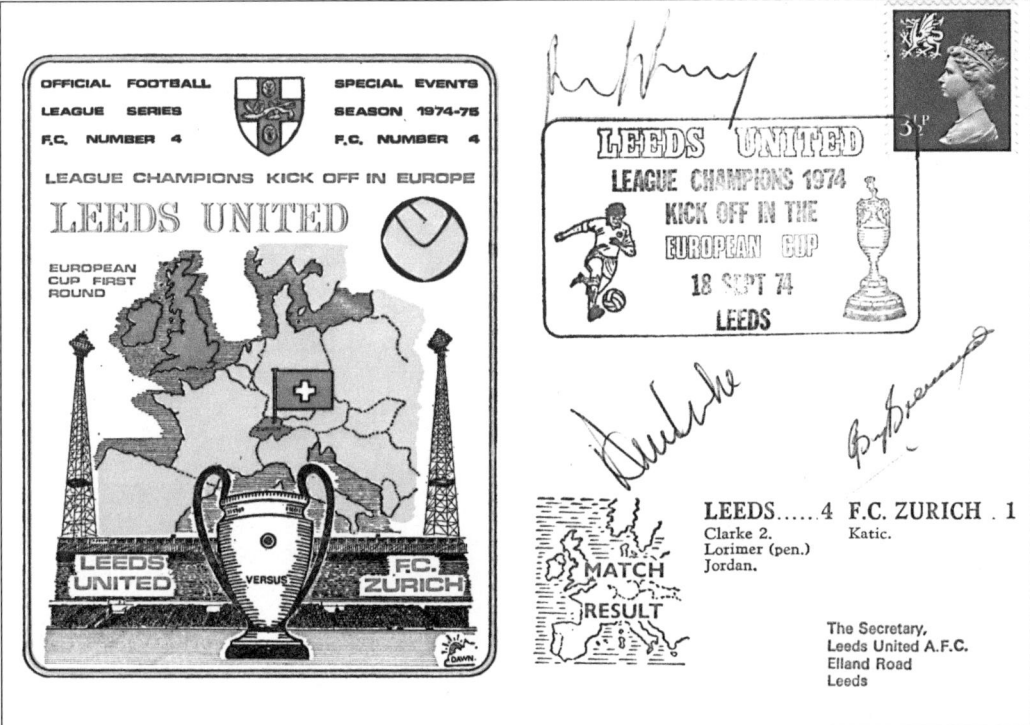

First day cover commemorating United's participation in the European Cup.

Jimmy Armfield's first foray into Europe as manager was a daunting trip to Hungarian League leaders Ujpest Dozsa. His inexperience in European competition proved irrelevant as United took the lead with a Lorimer thunderbolt. Leeds then showed their pedigree by overcoming Duncan McKenzie's sending off and Hungarian international Bene equalising with a penalty. Leeds carried the game to Dozsa and were rewarded when McQueen headed home just before half-time. Leeds controlled the match and were unlucky not to increase their lead. In the return game United ran out comfortable 3-0 winners, McQueen, Bremner and Yorath scoring. Note the psychedelic design of the match programme – this is not a printing error!

LEEDS UNITED

All White		Changes
1	David STEWART	
2	Paul REANEY	
3	Frank GRAY	
4	Billy BREMNER	
5	Paul MADELEY	
6	Norman HUNTER	
7	Peter LORIMER	
8	Allan CLARKE	
9	Joe JORDAN	
10	Johnny GILES	
11	Eddie GRAY	
12	Gordon McQUEEN	
13	Trevor CHERRY	
14	Terry YORATH	
15	Terry COOPER	
16	Glan LETHEREN	

R.S.O. ANDERLECHT

All Mauve		Changes
1	Jan RUITER	
2	Gilbert VAN BINST	
3	Hudo BROOS	
4	Erwin VAN DEN DAELE	
5	Jean THISSEN	
6	Francois VAN DER ELST	
7	Ludo COECK	
8	Torsten ANDERSEN	
9	Guido NICOLAES	
10	Paul VAN HIMST	
11	Robby RENSENBRINCK	
12		
13		
14		
15		
16		

Any two from five named substitutes can play.

Officials

Referee :
RUDI GLOCKNER

UEFA, the organising body of the European Champions Cup, pursue a policy of selecting match officials from the same country to officiate in all three European competitions. The officials work as a team, and will also officiate in the return leg in Belgium in a fortnight's time. The officials for this quarter-final tie are all from the German Democratic Republic (East Germany).

Rudi Glockner is one of Europe's most experienced and respected referees. He has handled a host of key European ties as well as many internationals and is no stranger to Leeds . . . he refereed the Fairs Cup tie against Bologna in April 1967 and the Final against Juventus in June, 1971.

Herr Glockner was a linesman for last summer's World Cup Final between West Germany and Holland.

Published by Leeds United Development Company Limited
Printed by : L. M. LEE (Printers) Ltd. Speedwell St., Leeds 6 Tel : 450661/2

Leeds drew crack Belgium side Anderlecht in the quarter-finals. This is the team sheet from the Elland Road clash. Anderlecht's line-up included such notable internationals as Francois Van der Elst, Paul Van Himst and Robbie Rensenbrink, but even they couldn't live with United who brushed them aside. The match was nearly postponed because a blanket of fog settled over the pitch as kick-off approached. Conditions hardly improved throughout, indeed when Jordan opened the scoring the Kop were heard to sing, 'All we are singing … is who scored the goal?' United added two more through McQueen and Lorimer. In the return, Bremner capped a magnificent personal performance with a wonderful lob to complete a 4-0 aggregate win. The Anderlecht 'keeper was so impressed by Bremner's skills that he went up to Bremner following the goal to shake him by the hand.

Leeds were renowned for meticulously planning their strategy for European trips, as this article from the Anderlecht programme describes. United's chief scout, Tony Collins, was despatched to check out hotel accommodation, travel details, and their opposition, all in the space of twenty-four hours. Perhaps this comprehensive review was one of the major reasons for United's decade of success in Europe.

All in a day's work …

They don't call Leeds United England's most thorough club for nothing. Ten years of the rigorous demands of top level competitions at home and abroad have seen the evolution of a 'spy' network second to none. So when United were drawn against Anderlecht in the European Cup in late January, priority one for the backroom staff was to mount an operation to find out all about the Belgian champions.

A couple of weeks ago, United's Chief Scout Tony Collins—whose in-depth dossier on Ujpest Dozsa for the second round tie was highly praised by manager Jimmy Armfield—had a whirlwind weekend to check on Anderlecht. The former Rochdale manager and Bristol City assistant manager had a demanding schedule . . . check on hotel accommodation, finalise travel details and run the critical eye over Anderlecht in the space of 24 hours.

We sent Leeds United Magazine photographer Peter Robinson out with Collins . . . his action pictures of the Anderlecht stars make an unusual centre page montage in this issue. The tight schedule began in the early hours of a Saturday morning when Collins left his Rochdale home for Manchester. He caught

the early train to London, took the tube to Spurs' White Hart Lane to take in the First Division game with Stoke, dashed to the West London air terminal after half time then caught his flight out of Heathrow to Brussels.

He was met by John Doorbar, (pictured above, right, with Collins outside the Holiday Inn in Brussels) the British Embassy official who has a long standing friendship with United's assistant manager Maurice Lindley and who took over the arrangements from there. Doorbar, First Secretary at the British Consulate in Brussels, acted as interpreter while Collins outlined United's hotel requirements, then drove the United 'super spy' to Ostend—some 80 miles away —in time for the game between Ostend and Anderlecht.

Anderlecht won 2—0 and Collins was able to make notes on what United should face tonight and in two week's time when they fly to Brussels for the return leg. "John Doorbar couldn't have been more helpful," says Collins. "He met me at the airport, took me to the hotel—normally a five minute drive but because of fog, it took us nearly an hour—then drove me to Ostend. At the game, he arranged for me to have a couple of team sheets— they don't have programmes in

Belgium; the teams are posted up on a notice board inside the ground—introduced me to officials of both teams then acted as interpreter again when the Belgian Press interviewed me after the game.

"John then managed to get me back to Brussels in time to catch the plane back to Manchester—even though the Anderlecht fans returning home had jammed the roads. I caught the plane with just a few minutes to spare. It wouldn't have been half as successful a trip without John's help. He's a mad keen football fan—he particularly follows Leeds, of course—and manages to put in a lot of work for his local club Mallois.

Collins' dossier on Anderlecht has been channelled into pre-match planning for tonight's game.

His whirlwind trip to Belgium finished late on the Sunday evening when friends picked him up from Manchester and drove him home. "It was a demanding 24 hours," he says, "but it was very worthwhile."

And the Tony Collins' assessment of Anderlecht . . . "A very, very good side. The fans are certainly in for a classic and we'll know we've got a match on our hands. It's going to be tough, but I think we can do it."

four

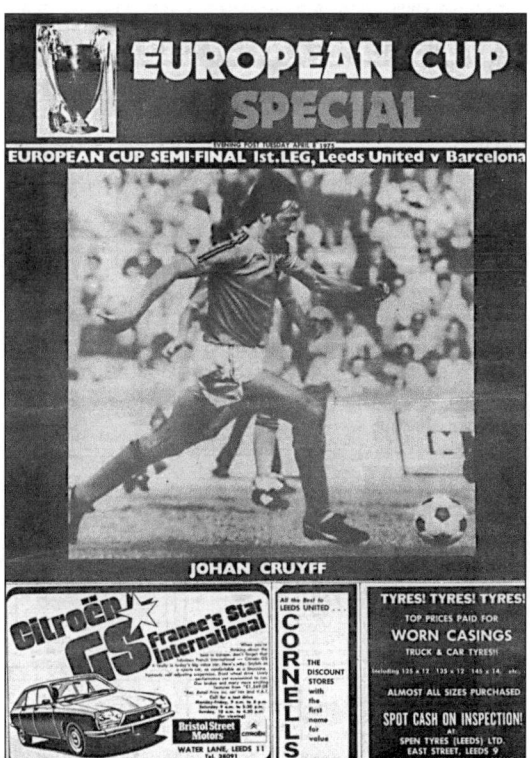

Leeds received the toughest draw possible in the semi-finals when they were paired with Spanish giants Barcelona, who included in their side one of football's all-time greats, Johan Cruyff. In the other semi-final Bayern Munich drew Saint-Etienne. *Above*: the *Yorkshire Evening Post* produced this European Cup Special. *Below*: A match ticket from the first-leg clash at Elland Road.

The capacity crowd crammed into Elland Road was to witness a gripping encounter in which the standard of football was exceptional. Leeds began impressively and Bremner fired home this unstoppable effort.

Halfway through the second half Asensi scored for Barcelona from a free kick, but their joy was short-lived as twelve minutes later Clarke (above) sent the crowd into delirium by finishing off a move involving Reaney and Jordan.

The only unsavoury incident of the tie involved Jordan and Barcelona 'keeper Sadurni, who clashed after Sadurni had made a brave save. Here, Cruyff acts as peacemaker between the two.

Bremner and Cruyff were never far apart throughout the match – United's skipper is pictured making his point as the tension mounts.

In the return United silenced 110,000 fanatical supporters with this early Lorimer strike. However, if Leeds thought Barcelona were finished they were wrong as the Catalonians poured forward. The remainder of the match saw Leeds desperately hanging on to their advantage. The inevitable equaliser arrived when Clares headed in Gallego's free kick and United's chances looked even bleaker when minutes later McQueen justifiably received his marching orders. In the end Leeds were indebted to brilliant defending and one superb Dave Stewart save from Cruyff to reach the final.

A delighted Norman Hunter leaves Barcelona's Nou Camp stadium after United's stunning 3-2 aggregate victory, easily one of their greatest results in Europe.

Leeds United, 1975 European Cup finalists. From left to right, back row: Paul Madeley, Norman Hunter, Trevor Cherry, Joe Jordan, Gordon McQueen, Dave Stewart, David Harvey, Eddie Gray, Allan Clarke, Paul Reaney. Front row: Peter Lorimer, Johnny Giles, Billy Bremner (captain), Terry Cooper, Mick Bates, Frank Gray, Terry Yorath.

Leeds United *v.* Bayern Munich, Parc de Prince Stadium, Paris, 28 May 1975.

United line-up for the pre-match formalities before facing two-time winners Bayern Munich. From left to right: Dave Stewart, Paul Reaney, Johnny Giles, Norman Hunter, Frank Gray, Peter Lorimer, Joe Jordan, Paul Madeley, Terry Yorath, Allan Clarke, Peter Hampton, Trevor Cherry, Eddie Gray, Glan Letheran, Duncan McKenzie, Billy Bremner.

Leeds dominated the first half, running Munich ragged. Following close efforts by Hunter and Lorimer, whose long-range shots fizzed past the post, they were extremely unlucky not to be awarded a penalty when Clarke had his legs whipped from under him by Beckenbauer on forty-three minutes. Incredibly the referee Mr Ktabdjian, less than ten yards away, failed to give the award, much to United's disbelief. The second half took a similar course when firstly Maier denied Bremner with a brilliant point-blank save, and then on sixty-six minutes when a linesman ruled out this unstoppable Lorimer volley because Bremner and Jordan had strayed offside. This latter incident was particularly galling, as the referee had initially awarded a goal.

United players lead the referee to the linesman in a vain attempt to overturn his decision. United never recovered from this blow and Bayern took full advantage scoring twice on the break through Roth and Muller.

Joe Jordan's expression at the end of the match says it all.

Madeley, Clarke and Bremner applaud their supporters before mayhem ensued. A number of United fans behaved abominably, rioting and challenging police to battle both inside and outside the stadium. It was inevitable the club would have to face the consequences for these actions and they did, receiving a European ban.

United players receive another warm homecoming outside Leeds Civic Hall. In truth, though, a magnificent era in Europe was over and this was a desperate way to end the ninth consecutive campaign. During that time they had reached five finals and two semi-finals – an astonishing record.

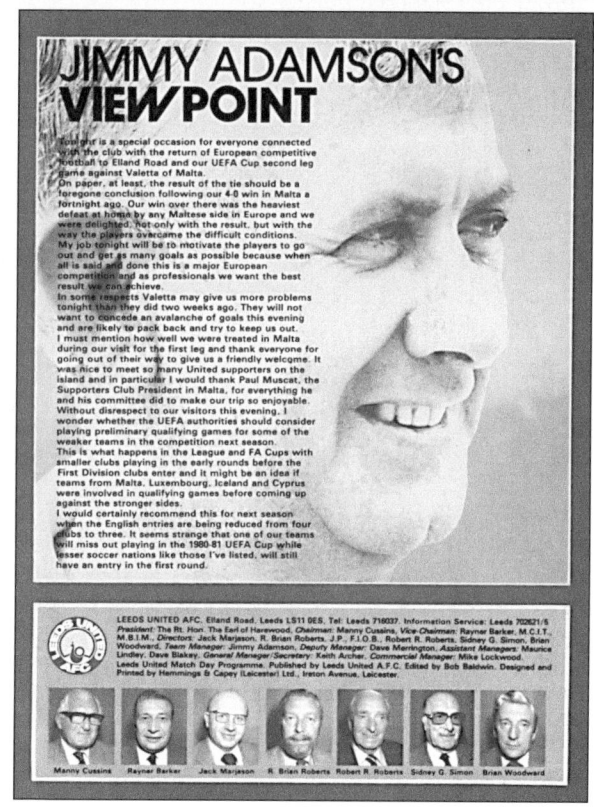

It took Leeds four seasons before they were back in Europe again. Here, United line up prior to the 1979/80 new season.

Drawn against Maltese side Valetta in the UEFA Cup, only Paul Madeley and Eddie Gray remained from the European Cup final team. United were thankful for Arthur Graham's hat-trick in a 4-0 victory at the Gzira Stadium. In the return, goals from Alan Curtis, Ray Hankin and Paul Hart confirmed a 7-0 stroll. New manager Jimmy Adamson gave his views in the match programme prior to the return at Elland Road.

JIMMY ADAMSON'S VIEWPOINT

Tonight is a special occasion for everyone connected with the club with the return of European competitive football to Elland Road and our UEFA Cup second leg game against Valetta of Malta.

On paper, at least, the result of the tie should be a foregone conclusion following our 4-0 win in Malta a fortnight ago. Our win over there was the heaviest defeat at home by any Maltese side in Europe and we were delighted, not only with the result, but with the way the players overcame the difficult conditions.

My job tonight will be to motivate the players to go out and get as many goals as possible because when all is said and done this is a major European competition and as professionals we want the best result we can achieve.

In some respects Valetta may give us more problems tonight than they did two weeks ago. They will not want to concede an avalanche of goals this evening and are likely to pack back and try to keep us out.

I must mention how well we were treated in Malta during our visit for the first leg and thank everyone for going out of their way to give us a friendly welcome. It was nice to meet so many United supporters on the island and in particular I would thank Paul Muscat, the Supporters Club President in Malta, for everything he and his committee did to make our trip so enjoyable.

Without disrespect to our visitors this evening, I wonder whether the UEFA authorities should consider playing preliminary qualifying games for some of the weaker teams in the competition next season.

This is what happens in the League and FA Cups with smaller clubs playing in the early rounds before the First Division clubs enter and it might be an idea if teams from Malta, Luxemburg, Iceland and Cyprus were involved in qualifying games before coming up against the stronger sides.

I would certainly recommend this for next season when the English entries are being reduced from four clubs to three. It seems strange that one of our teams will miss out playing in the 1980-81 UEFA Cup while lesser soccer nations like those I've listed, will still have an entry in the first round.

LEEDS UNITED AFC, Elland Road, Leeds LS11 0ES, Tel. Leeds 716037. Information Service: Leeds 702621/5. President: The Rt. Hon. The Earl of Harewood, Chairman: Manny Cussins, Vice-Chairman: Raynor Barker, M.C.I.T., M.B.I.M., Directors: Jack Marjason, R. Brian Roberts, J.P., F.I.O.B., Robert R. Roberts, Sidney G. Simon, Brian Woodward, Team Manager: Jimmy Adamson, Deputy Manager: Dave Merrington, Assistant Managers: Maurice Lindley, Dave Blakey, General Manager/Secretary: Keith Archer, Commercial Manager: Mike Lockwood. Leeds United Match Day Programme. Published by Leeds United A.F.C. Edited by Bob Baldwin. Designed and Printed by Hemmings & Capey (Leicester) Ltd., Irston Avenue, Leicester.

Manny Cussins Raynor Barker Jack Marjason R. Brian Roberts Robert R. Roberts Sidney G. Simon Brian Woodward

The return with Valetta marked the debut of John Lukic, who would remarkably play in United's next two European campaigns stretching over sixteen years. Goalscorers on the night were Arthur Graham (left) and Paul Hart (below). In the second round, United's European dream ended with a 4-0 aggregate defeat at the hands of Universitatea Craiova.

Five

Wilko, George and O'Leary

1993-2000

Leeds United's squad for the 1995/96 campaign. From left to right, back row: David White, Brian Deane, Carlton Palmer, John Lukic, David Wetherall, Mark Beeney, Philomen Masinga, Lucas Radebe, Paul Beesley. Middle row: Mike Hennigan (assistant manager), Matthew Smithard, Mark Ford, Noel Whelan, Robert Bowman, Mark Tinkler, Andy Couzens, Kevin Sharp, Tony Dorigo, Nigel Worthington, David O'Leary, David Williams (coach), Geoff Ladley (physiotherapist). Front row: Rod Wallace, Tony Yeboah, Gary McAllister (captain), Howard Wilkinson (manager), John Pemberton, Gary Speed, Gary Kelly.

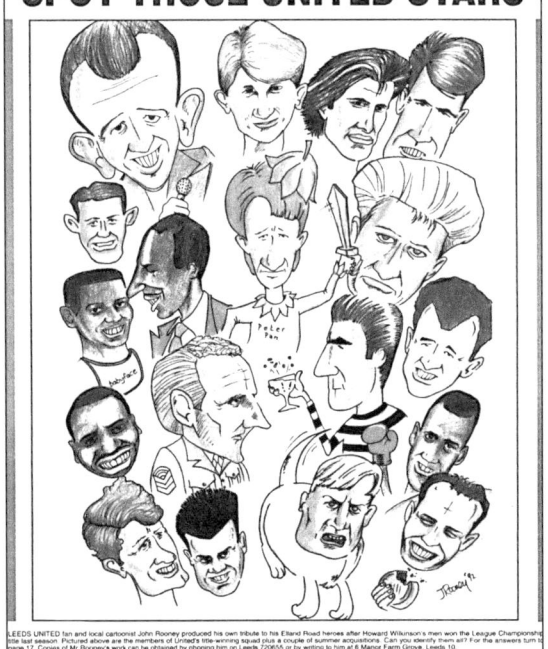

SPOT THOSE UNITED STARS

LEEDS UNITED fan and local cartoonist John Rooney produced his own tribute to his Elland Road heroes after Howard Wilkinson's men won the League Championship title last season. Pictured above are the members of United's title-winning squad plus a couple of summer acquisitions. Can you identify them all? For the answers turn to page 17. Copies of Mr Rooney's work can be obtained by phoning him on Leeds 720655 or by writing to him at 6 Manor Farm Grove, Leeds 10.

Above left: Fresh from their First Division Championship success, Leeds entered the 1992/93 European Cup with a first round clash against surprise German Champions VFB Stuttgart. Here, their squad is caricatured by local cartoonist Rooney. *Above right and below:* In the first leg at the Necker Stadion, United impressed for forty-five minutes and were unlucky not to be ahead at the break. However, all was to change soon after the restart as an injured Eric Cantona gifted the Germans a goal with a wayward pass, Walter chipping home. Two further goals by Walter and Buck left Leeds with a mountain to climb – never before had they been asked to make up a three-goal deficit to advance to the next round. Here, United's match programme shows David Batty and David Rocastle (making his debut) in action during the match in Germany.

Only 20,457 fans witnessed an unbelievable return leg. United lifted the crowd by attacking from the start and were rewarded when Speed volleyed home. Committed to going forwards, Leeds were rocked when Buck equalised from a rare counter-attack. Undeterred, United retook the lead from a McAllister penalty after Lee Chapman had been impeded. Unbelievably the impossible seemed attainable when Cantona (sixty-nine minutes – shown here) and Chapman (eighty minutes) scored further goals. Stuttgart's manager panicked and brought on a fourth foreign player, Yugoslav substitute Simanic, with seven minutes remaining. Although Stuggart held out for an away goals victory, within twenty-four hours Leeds were reinstated after Stuttgart admitted breaking UEFA's foreign player rule during the substitution. UEFA ordered a third match to be played at Barcelona's Nou Camp stadium.

READY FOR TAKE-OFF

LEEDS UNITED'S Carl Shutt, Jon Newsome and Chris Fairclough pictured on their departure for Barcelona for their European Cup first round re-match with Stuttgart. United, of course, won 2-1 and if they can despatch Glasgow Rangers in the second round tonight, they can look forward to a few more trips to the continent as the European Cup competition splits into its two league format.

Days after UEFA's decision Leeds head for Barcelona.

On Friday 9 October 1992, United lined up at the Nou Camp with just 10,000 fans filling the 120,000 capacity stadium. In a controlled opening United seized the initiative with this cracking twenty-five-yard effort from skipper Gordon Strachan.

A delighted Strachan receives congratulations from his team-mates.

United's lead lasted seven minutes, as Stuttgart midfielder Golke headed home Strehnel's low centre, and the match remained deadlocked until fifteen minutes from time when Howard Wilkinson made an inspired substitution. On the day before his thirty-first birthday, Carl Shutt replaced an ineffective Cantona and within sixty seconds charged down Buck's attempted clearance before gliding past Schaefers and firing home this angled drive for the winner on a glorious night.

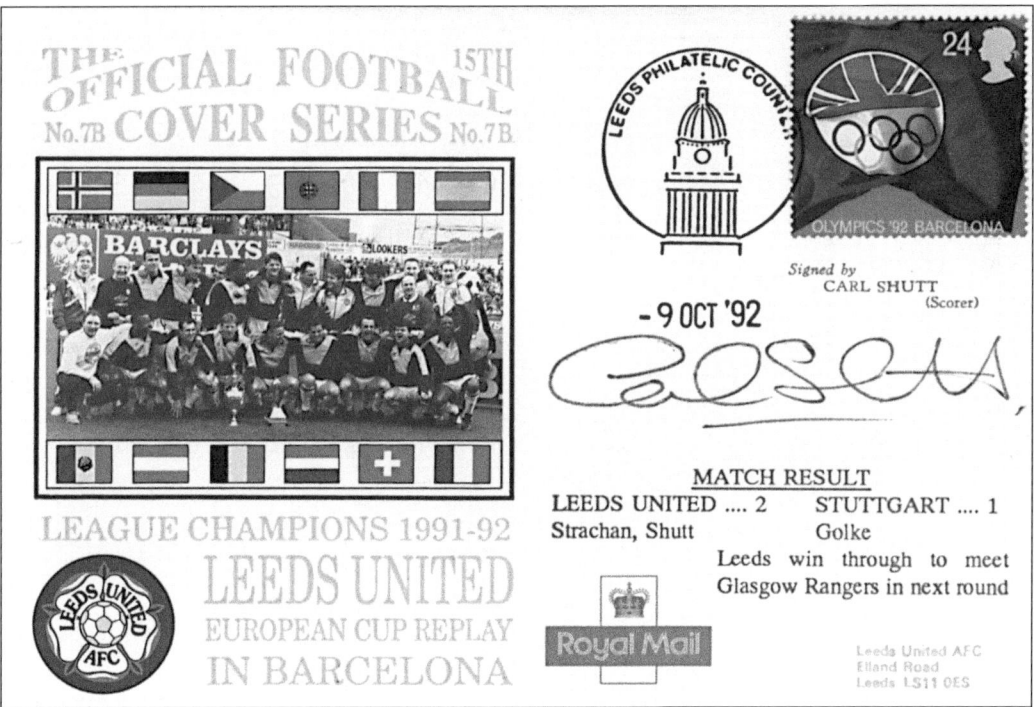

This first day cover commemorates United's win in Barcelona.

Victory over Stuttgart earned Leeds a mouth-watering tie against Glasgow Rangers. The media hype was unprecedented as United made the short trip to Glasgow for a tie dubbed the 'Battle of Britain'. A strange atmosphere greeted Leeds as both clubs had agreed that only home supporters would be allowed for the ties due to the incredible demand for tickets. Within sixty-six seconds United had silenced the crowd with a precise McAllister volley, following a poor clearance from Strachan's corner. Here, United players celebrate the goal. Unfortunately, Rangers fought back and took the lead before the interval following a terrible error by Lukic, who punched Ian Durrant's corner into his own net, and an Ally McCoist strike on thirty-seven minutes. Try as they might Leeds failed to find an equaliser.

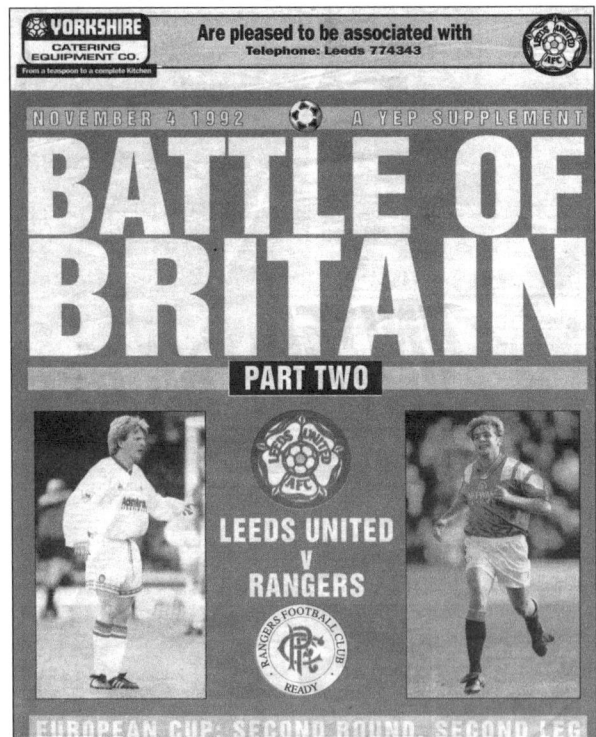

In the return the Scots stunned Leeds after two minutes when Mark Hateley caught Lukic out with an unstoppable thirty-five-yard strike. McCoist's goal on the hour sealed United's fate. The match finished 2-1, Cantona scoring for Leeds. The *Yorkshire Evening Post* brought out this special edition for the game.

One person was responsible for United's return to European action in 1995/96 – Tony Yeboah. His dozen goals towards the end of the previous season had enabled United to pip Newcastle for the last UEFA Cup spot. Yeboah is seen here looking confident before departing for Leeds' first round encounter with a star-studded AS Monaco.

United's match programme for the return records highlights from the first leg, including in the centre the first goal of Yeboah's hat-trick after just three minutes. The match ended 3-0. The scoreline proved sufficient to take Leeds through to the next round despite a 1-0 reverse at Elland Road, where man of the match for United, John Lukic, saved his side time and again.

Leeds drew one of the tournament favourites in the second round, Dick Advocaat's awesome PSV Eindhoven. PSV's squad, which included Cocu, Wim Jonk, Arthur Numan, Luke Nilis and a young nineteen-year-old Brazilian called Ronaldo, tore United to shreds in the first leg at Elland Road. Leeds were simply outclassed. Twice two goals behind in the first half, they rallied briefly, pulling the game level just after the interval before Eindhoven once again raised their game to record a 5-3 triumph. This was United's 100th tie in Europe and their heaviest defeat. Here, McAllister battles hard as he tries to create an opening at Elland Road.

Speed and Whelan celebrate the Welshman's goal in the 5-3 defeat. In the return PSV cantered to a 3-0 victory on the night and an 8-3 aggregate win.

Whilst George Graham's first full season in charge at Leeds brought qualification to the UEFA Cup, by the time United lined up against CS Maritimo at Elland Road speculation surrounding his future took centre stage, the game itself proving nothing more than a sideshow. Despite dominating play Leeds were thankful for this goal from Jimmy Floyd Hasselbaink's free kick after eighty-six minutes.

'Jimmy' leads the celebrations. The return leg was dire, with Leeds appearing happy for the match to be settled on penalties after Suarez had equalised on the stroke of half-time. United won the tie 4-1 in a penalty shoot out as Maritimo buckled under the pressure, Lee Sharpe scoring the deciding penalty. As the players celebrated, George Graham confirmed to chairman Peter Ridsdale his intention to resign and join Spurs.

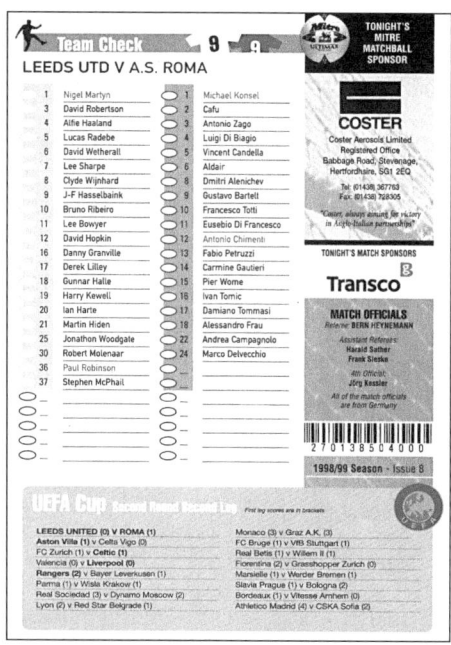

Could there have been a more demanding fixture than playing AS Roma at the Olympic Stadium to kick-off David O'Leary's managerial career in Europe? Leeds played out of their skin, but unfortunately with little luck. A goal down from an early Delvecchio strike, United dug deep and were unlucky as first Bruno Ribeiro and then Gunnar Halle both struck an upright. Nigel Martyn was magnificent and Leeds held on for the last thirty-five minutes after Ribeiro received a second yellow card. The performance won United rave reviews. This is the team sheet in the return leg's match programme.

In the return Leeds suffered a night of frustration and failed to overturn their one-goal deficit. Roma's defence proved impregnable, even when reduced to ten men after Wome was dismissed shortly before the interval. Sharpe and Bowyer both missed chances which from the stands looked easier to score. In reality Leeds produced little, the depleted Italians winning comfortably on aggregate. Here, Bowyer and McPhail fight for control in midfield. The League campaign again brought European qualification, something which seemed inconceivable at that stage of the season. This was due in no small measure to the managerial partnership of David O'Leary and Eddie Gray, who by blooding the cream of United's youth alongside experienced internationals produced an exciting mix of flair and creativity.

Leeds United first team squad, 1999/2000. From left to right, back row: Robert Molenaar, Michael Bridges, Jonathon Woodgate, Nigel Martyn, Michael Duberry, Paul Robinson, Eirik Bakke, Alf-Inge Haaland, David Hopkin. Middle row: Sean Hardy (kit manager), Bruno Ribeiro, Ian Harte, David Batty, Gary Kelly, Danny Mills, Jimmy Hasselbaink, Eddie Gray (assistant manager), David Swift (physiotherapist). Front row: Stephen McPhail, Alan Smith, Harry Kewell, Peter Ridsdale (chairman), Lucas Radebe (captain), David O'Leary (manager), Lee Bowyer, Matthew Jones, Martin Hiden.

The 2000 UEFA Cup first round draw pitted Leeds against Yugoslavian Champions, Partizan Belgrade, preliminary round losers in the Champions League. There was confusion over the venue for Partizan's 'home' leg as the European Union had severed sporting links with Yugoslavia. After two weeks' negotiation, Partizan were forced to hold the tie in Heerenveen, Holland. Recovering from going a goal down after twenty minutes, Leeds fought back to win 3-1 with two goals from Bowyer and a comically acrobatic overhead volley by skipper Radebe. Leeds were also thankful to Martyn, who saved a penalty after a Radebe foul tackle. Batty is pictured here scrapping for possession as Woodgate looks on.

O'Leary thanks supporters at the end of the match after his side had taken a giant step towards the next round. In the return a solo effort from Huckerby ensured Leeds' place in the next round.

Lokomotiv Moscow felt the full force of a scintillating display from O'Leary's team as Leeds won 4-1, Bowyer (two), Smith and Kewell scoring. Here, Bowyer celebrates one of his brace of goals with Bridges and Woodgate.

Smith wheels away after his athletic bicycle kick brought United's third goal. The return in Moscow, United's first match in Russia, proved to be a stroll as three first half goals from Bridges (two) and Harte (penalty) completed a 7-1 aggregate win. Although they showed such dominance, O'Leary attempted to play down his side's chances of progression in the competition. O'Leary particularly bemoaned the fact that Champions League third-placed teams were allowed and about to enter the UEFA Cup.

While the *Yorkshire Evening Post* choose to lead on the only disappointing note from United's clash with Lokomotiv, the suspension of captain Lucas Radebe from the next match, the main picture concentrates on two-goal hero Michael Bridges.

Castleford Tigers
Season tickets 2000
Best value in Super League
Phone: 01977 555703

yep.sport@ypn.co.uk

SPORT

M.H.F. BED WAREHOUSE
100's of Beds at Ridiculously low prices
Tel: 0113 246 5444
Unit 4 Roseville Rd., Leeds
(opp. Appleyards)

FRIDAY 5 NOVEMBER 1999

● GOAL-DEN BOY: Michael Bridges celebrates his double, above, while Lucas Radebe salutes the travelling United fans, left.   PICTURES: MARK BICKERDIKE

RADEBE'S EURO BLOW

United skipper Lucas is banned from the next round

BY PHIL ROSTRON

LEEDS UNITED cruised through to the third round of the UEFA Cup in Russia last night and skipper Lucas Radebe beamed: "The lads can go forward without me, and they will."

Radebe will miss the first leg of the next stage after receiving his third yellow card in European competition this season, but he was overjoyed with the 3-0 second round, second leg victory over Lokomotive Moscow on an icy night miles from home. The comprehensive victory gave United an emphatic 7-1 aggregate beating of the second best side in Russia behind their neighbours, Spartak.

And Radebe said: "I'm very disappointed to have been booked, but there is nothing you can do about it.

"You are going into a tackle thinking that you must avoid contact with the opposing player, but the nature of the game is that sometimes you will.

"You get punished and at the time you don't really think of the consequences. It is only when you get into the dressing room at the end of the game that you realise the enormity in situations like this. It will be hard for me to sit out the first leg, but the lads can cope without me."

Radebe played a marvellous defensive role in a rock solid Leeds performance and one which, frankly, confirmed them in a different class to their Russian opposition.

United boss David O'Leary is aware that the competition will get more fierce from the next stage when the Champions' League drop-outs come into the UEFA Cup.

Turn to Page 53

Match report: Pages 58&59

Turn to Page 53

Ironically, United faced an immediate return trip to Moscow to face Champions League failures Spartak Moscow in the third round. Moscow at the end of November was a far colder place than on their last visit. From the moment the team touched down, Leeds officials were concerned at the state of the frozen Dynamo stadium, which O'Leary described as 'dangerous and unplayable', a description which Swedish referee Anders Frisk eventually agreed with. For the second time in United's campaign UEFA were forced to rearrange an opening tie, on this occasion to Sofia in Bulgaria. Relations between the two camps soured, Spartak accusing Leeds of being 'soft and running scared' as they flew home. Next day the *Yorkshire Evening Post* summed up United's feelings.

● IN FROM THE COLD: Leeds United manager David O'Leary tries to conduct a training session on the frozen pitch in Moscow last night, but it last just ten minutes in the farcical conditions. PICTURES: BRUCE ROLLINSON

A FARCE!

UEFA Cup tie dramatically postponed

BY PHIL ROSTRON
IN MOSCOW

LEEDS United's UEFA Cup tie with Spartak Moscow turned into a farce today when the game was dramatically postponed just hours before kick-off.

United were due to face the Russians in a third round, first leg tie at 5pm British time, but following meetings between match officials, UEFA and representatives of both clubs, the match was called off due to the frozen state of the pitch.

Swedish referee Anders Frisk carried out a 2pm inspection (11am British time) and confirmed the surface was too dangerous to play on.

He said: "The match will not be played tonight. Regulations then stipulate that the game be played tomorrow. But the Russians cannot 100% guarantee the weather and the pitch for tomorrow either, so we have postponed the game.

"Both clubs are now in negotiations to fix a new date and venue. It must be in a place that can be 100% guaranteed.

Slamming

"It's quite obvious the pitch was too hard and there is also a question about the weather, which was also a consideration for tomorrow. It's also due to be very cold tomorrow.

"It was for the safety of the players, the referee and for UEFA that this match has been called off."

United attempted to train at the ground last night, but that had to be aborted with manager David O'Leary slamming the state of the pitch as 'dangerous' and 'unplayable'.

The 18-man squad arrived at the stadium for a 6pm training session last night in temperatures of minus 15 degrees to find the undersoil heating had not been switched on and the pitch was an ice rink.

It now seems highly likely that the scheduled return clash at Elland Road on December 9 will become the first leg.

There is no chance of the teams meeting next week with United taking on Southampton on Sunday, travelling to Leicester in the Worthington Cup on Tuesday before making a trip to Pride Park and an FA Carling Premiership match with Derby a week on Saturday.

More than 500 United fans made the trip to Moscow and will no doubt be demanding compensation.

● ROCK SOLID: The pitch in the Dynamo Stadium in Moscow

YORKSHIRE EVENING POST SPORT STARTS TODAY WITH RACING ON PAGE 62

YORKSHIRE EVENING POST SPORT STARTS TODAY WITH RACING ON PAGE 62

With Lucas Radebe suspended, Gary Kelly leads out United on a cold Bulgarian evening.

Leeds started magnificently, Kewell striking the woodwork before intercepting a back pass to give United the lead from an acute angle. The Aussie is pictured here wheeling away in celebration. The game turned after Bridges was injured following a clash with Russian 'keeper Filimonov. The Russians then took control, scoring twice through Schirko and Robson. After this Leeds were fortunate to prevent Spartak taking a stranglehold on the tie, escaping with only a 2-1 defeat.

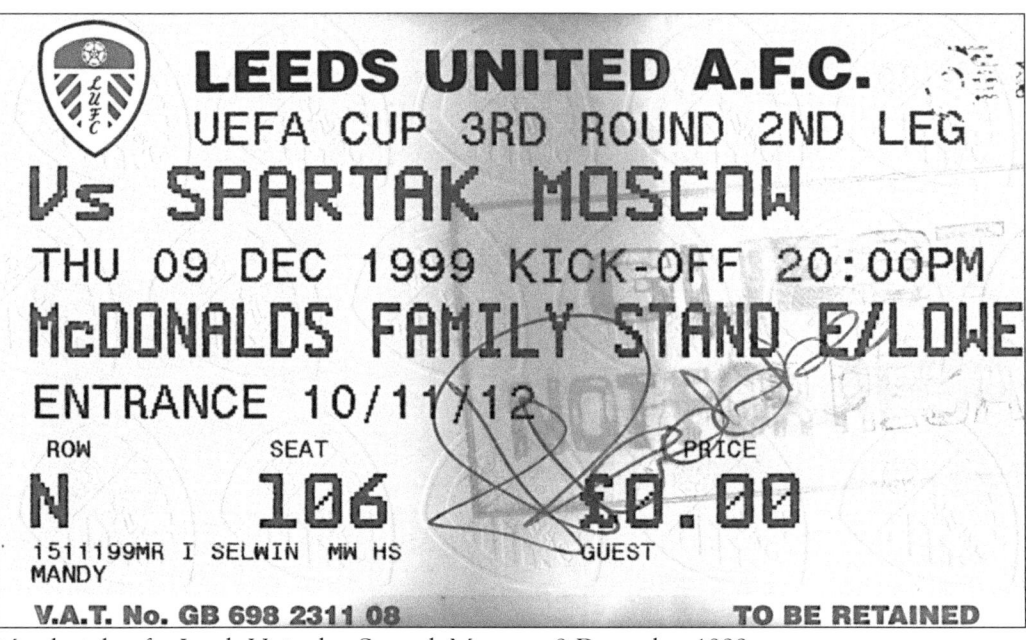

LEEDS UNITED A.F.C.
UEFA CUP 3RD ROUND 2ND LEG
Vs SPARTAK MOSCOW
THU 09 DEC 1999 KICK-OFF 20:00PM
McDONALDS FAMILY STAND B/LOWE
ENTRANCE 10/11/12

ROW	SEAT	PRICE
N	106	£0.00

1511199MR I SELWIN MW HS
MANDY   GUEST

V.A.T. No. GB 698 2311 08   TO BE RETAINED

Match ticket for Leeds United *v.* Spartak Moscow, 9 December 1999.

The return leg with Spartak was a thrilling encounter, played in an electric atmosphere. Leeds knew one goal would take them through and never panicked, even though their technically superior opponents dominated possession. Both sides had opportunities to break the deadlock, but didn't. Just as the most optimistic of United fans began to wonder if a goal would arrive, Radebe powerfully headed home McPhail's corner six minutes from time, after Spartak's substitute 'keeper Smetanin had misjudged it. Despite a couple of anxious moments Leeds held firm to book a place in the fourth round on the away goals rule. At the final whistle O'Leary punched the air in celebration before turning round to smugly glare at the vanquished Moscow bench whose coach, Roman Tsev, had orchestrated a campaign to intimidate his young team.

In the fourth round Leeds again faced AS Roma. United arrived at the Olympic Stadium determined to avenge the previous season's defeat, but knew they would be severely tested by a much-strengthened Roma squad, which included new signings Nakata and Montella. Undaunted, Leeds attacked from the start and were unlucky when Bakke had his second minute effort saved by Antonioli. After this Roma dominated, going close several times with Totti pulling the strings. Leeds were indebted to a magnificent display in goal by Martyn, who produced a string of world class saves to keep Roma at bay. *Above*: Martyn leads the players' applause at the end of the game, which finished 0-0. *Below*: A match ticket for the return leg.

LEEDS UNITED A.F.C.
UEFA CUP 4TH ROUND 2ND LEG
Vs AS ROMA
THU 09 MAR 2000 KICK-OFF 20:00PM
McDONALDS FAMILY STAND E/LOWE
ENTRANCE 10/11/12

ROW	SEAT	PRICE
N	107	£11.25
1301200SAFFER DANNY		FAMILY PACKAGE

V.A.T. No. GB 698 2311 08   TO BE RETAINED

YORKSHIRE
Evening Post

www.yorkshireeveningpost.co.uk

FRIDAY 10 MARCH 2000 30P

LEEDS NORTH EDITION

HARRY COOL!

Kewell's the hero on night of glory

LEEDS UNITED 1 ROMA 0 PAGES 52-55

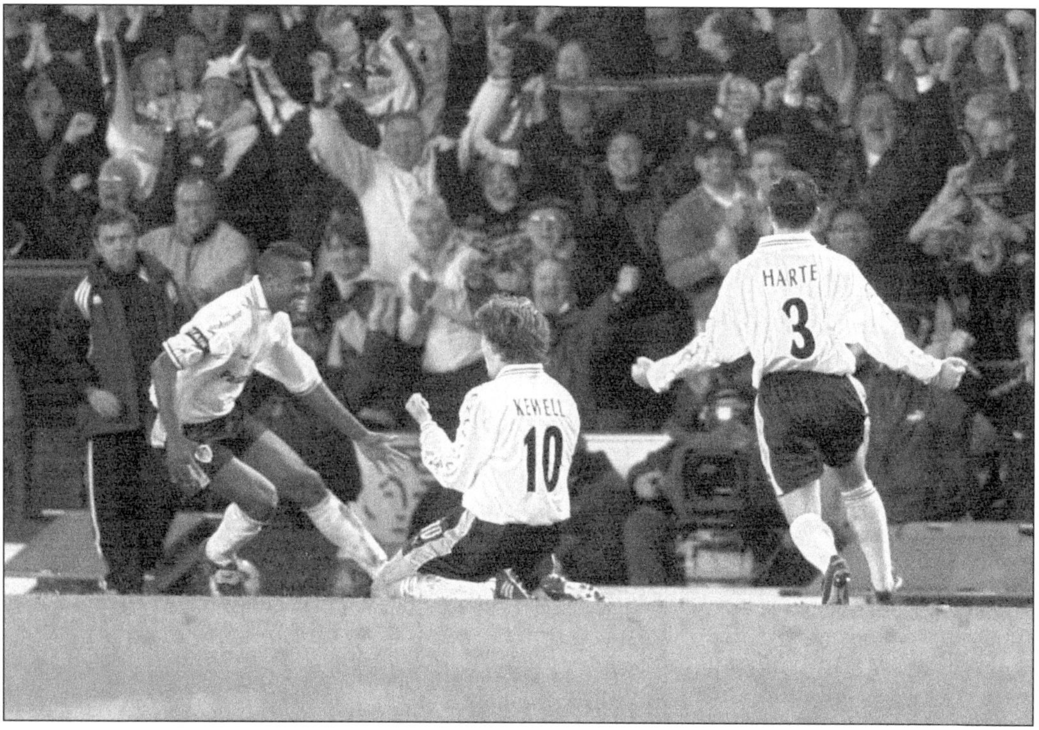

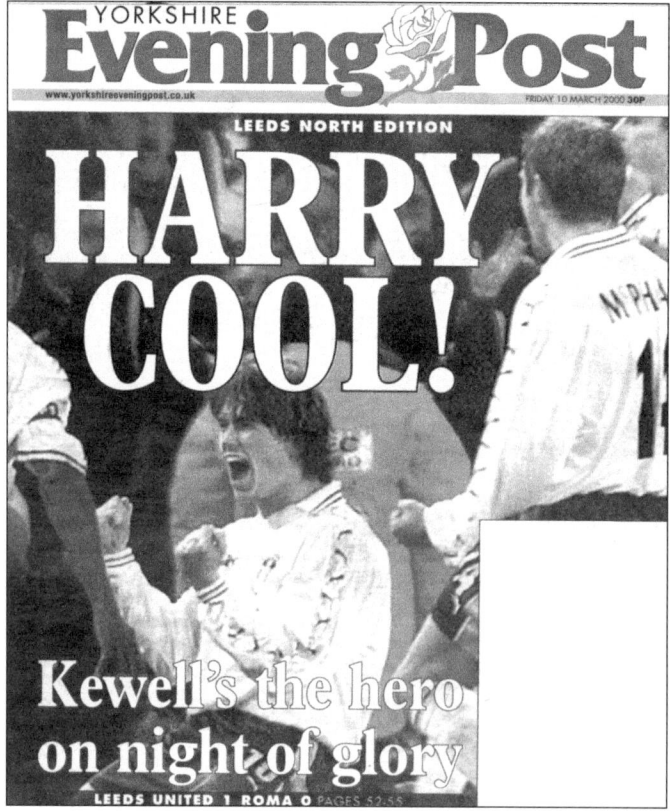

The return match with Roma was always going to be a huge test for O'Leary's young team. Another capacity crowd was to witness a tension-filled ninety minutes. Knowing one slip would cost them dear, Leeds needed their defence to remain solid. From the early stages Roma dominated possession, wasting several half-chances. However, Radebe and in particular Haaland were immense. On the hour Haaland charged forward, causing commotion in Roma's defence. A square ball from Bowyer found Kewell twenty-five-yards out, who steadied himself before firing home, the ball cannoning off the goalkeeper and the underside of the bar. *Above*: Kewell sinks to his knees after scoring the decisive goal. *Below*: The *Yorkshire Evening Post*'s coverage of the moment the next day.

United's defence held firm as Roma threw everything at them and as the game entered stoppage time Roma's frustrations finally boiled over. Here, Zago (3), Aldair (6) and Candela (32) exchange pleasantries with Smith and Kewell. Following this incident Zago and Candela were red-carded for head-butting Smith and Huckerby.

At the final whistle O'Leary immediately ran to his players to celebrate what he later described as, 'a wonderful achievement and the best of my managerial career so far'.

Seven days after the Roma triumph, Elland Road was full again for the quarter-final clash with Slavia Prague. In a one-sided encounter Leeds ripped apart their Czech opponents. In truth the one-goal advantage Leeds had at the interval was poor reward for their efforts. *Above*: The goal itself was a gem. Created by Bowyer's tenacity and vision, his pin-point through-ball found Jason Wilcox's perfectly timed run and he crashed the ball over the advancing 'keeper into the net. *Below*: Wilcox celebrates his marvellous strike.

After the interval two further goals from Kewell (shown above) and Bowyer sealed a satisfactory evening for Leeds, even though the difference between the sides was far greater than the 3-0 scoreline suggested.

Kewell congratulates Bowyer after his strike gave United a three-goal cushion. In Prague a clinical strike from Kewell effectively ended the tie, though Prague did fight back to win 2-1 on the night. Leeds, however, were comfortably through 4-2 on aggregate to claim their first European semi-final spot for twenty-five years.

In the blackest day in the club's history, two life-long Leeds supporters, Christopher Loftus and Kevin Speight, were murdered in Taksim Square, Istanbul, the night before the first leg with Galatasaray. The two were amongst a group of Leeds fans set-upon by a gang of Turkish hooligans bearing machetes, knives, and chair and table legs. In the hours that followed, the management team tried to protect the players but were unable to prevent death threats being received. Leeds chairman, Peter Ridsdale, spent the night comforting friends and relations of the dead and injured. Later he reluctantly agreed with UEFA and Galatasaray officials that the game, a total irrelevance following the events of the night before, should go ahead. The club immediately cancelled planned flights from Yeadon Airport to prevent other fans from travelling. Security for the match was incredibly tight, armoured vehicles escorting United's coach and those of the supporters and English press to the stadium. Inside the ground the atmosphere was awful and United entered the stadium shielded by the Turkish Army. Galatasaray refused to wear black armbands and observe a minute's silence – to the astonishment of United. In response the 700 visiting supporters turned their back on the pitch just prior to kick-off to hold their own silent vigil and were dignified throughout. When the match finally started, unsurprisingly Leeds began badly, two defensive errors allowing Sukur and Capone to score. Leeds wasted numerous opportunities to score an away goal in the second half when Bridges, Kewell and McPhail should have scored but didn't. In light of events the previous evening, however, the result didn't matter one iota as United and their supporters made a hasty departure straight after the game.

Back in Leeds, the city and indeed the whole of the footballing community grieved. Billy Bremner's statue outside Elland Road became the focal point for fans. Flowers, scarves and shirts from throughout the UK, including those from the fiercest of rivals, adorned the statue and gates at the club. To reduce tensions for the return leg Peter Ridsdale wanted Turkish fans banned. UEFA dithered for ten days and even contemplated switching the tie to a neutral venue as the Turks preferred. During this time Leeds' fans grief turned to anger as UEFA charged United with misconduct for having four players booked in the first leg. Their insensitivity was astonishing. Eventually UEFA agreed with Ridsdale. *Above*: On the field Leeds kept going and this picture shows United's players united in grief during the minute's silence at Villa Park four days after the tragedy. *Below*: On a highly charged night at Elland Road, Galatasaray players shake hands with United prior to kick off.

A few minutes into the return leg, United's dream of their first European final for twenty-five years was effectively over when Woodgate conceded a penalty from which Hagi scored. Leeds fought gallantly and briefly raised hopes when Bakke headed home a Wilcox corner. Any dreams of a comeback, however, were dashed three minutes from the interval when Sukur outfoxed the Leeds defence to score. Moment's later Kewell was sent off for an innocuous foul on Popescu, who feigned injury and fooled the referee. This act backfired on the Turks when Emre was sent off immediately afterwards for fouling Bowyer. United equalised for a second time when Bakke headed home another Wilcox corner, but for all their efforts Leeds could not find another goal. United had lost the tie 4-2 on aggregate, their European dream was over for another year. *Above and left*: Bakke scores his first of the night before celebrating.

European Roll of Honour

European Cup

1969/70	Semi-Finalists
1974/75	Finalists
1992/93	Second Round

European Cup Winners' Cup

1972/73	Finalists

Inter-Cities Fairs Cup

1965/66	Semi-Finalists
1966/67	Finalists
1967/68	Winners
1968/69	Quarter-Finals
1970/71	Winners

UEFA Cup

1971/72	First Round
1973/74	Third Round
1979/80	Second Round
1995/96	Second Round
1998/99	Second Round
1999/2000	Semi-Finalists

European Statistics: 1965-2000

1965/66   INTER-CITIES FAIRS CUP

FIRST ROUND First Leg
Leeds United 2 (Bremner, Peacock) Torino 1
Sprake, Reaney, Madeley, Bremner, Charlton, Hunter, Giles, Lorimer, Peacock, Collins, Cooper

FIRST ROUND Second Leg
Torino 0 Leeds United 0
Sprake, Reaney, Madeley, Bremner, Charlton, Hunter, Giles, Lorimer, Peacock, Collins, Cooper

Leeds United win on aggregate 2-1

SECOND ROUND First Leg
SC Leipzig 1 Leeds United 2 (Lorimer, Bremner)
Sprake, Reaney, Bell, Bremner, Charlton, Hunter, Storrie, Lorimer, Madeley, Giles, O'Grady

SECOND ROUND Second Leg
Leeds United 0 SC Leipzig 0
Sprake, Reaney, Bell, Bremner, Charlton, Hunter, Storrie, Lorimer, Peacock, Giles, O'Grady

Leeds United win on aggregate 2-1

THIRD ROUND First Leg
Leeds United 1 (Lorimer) Valencia 1
Sprake, Reaney, Bell, Bremner, Charlton, Hunter, Storrie, Lorimer, Belfitt, Giles, O'Grady

THIRD ROUND Second Leg
Valencia 0 Leeds United 1 (O'Grady)
Sprake, Reaney, Bell, Bremner, Charlton, Hunter, Storrie, Lorimer, Madeley, Giles, O'Grady

Leeds United win on aggregate 2-1

QUARTER-FINAL First Leg
Leeds United 4 (Cooper, Bell, Storrie, Bremner) Ujpest Dozsa 1
Sprake, Reaney, Bell, Bremner, Charlton, Hunter, O'Grady, Lorimer, Storrie, Giles, Cooper

QUARTER-FINAL Second Leg
Ujpest Dozsa 1 Leeds United 1 (Lorimer)
Sprake, Reaney, Bell, Bremner, Charlton, Hunter, O'Grady, Lorimer, Storrie, Giles, Cooper

Leeds United win on aggregate 5-2

SEMI-FINAL First Leg
Real Zaragoza 1 Leeds United 0
Sprake, Reaney, Bell, Bremner, Charlton, Hunter, Greenhoff, Gray E., Storrie, Giles, Johanneson

SEMI-FINAL Second Leg
Leeds United 2 (Johanneson, Charlton) Real Zaragoza 1
Sprake, Reaney, Bell, Bremner, Charlton, Hunter, Greenhoff, Gray E., Storrie, Giles, Johanneson

Match tied on aggregate 2-2, Leeds United won toss of disc to decide venue

SEMI-FINAL PLAY-OFF
Leeds United 1 (Charlton) Real Zaragoza 3
Sprake, Reaney, Bell, Bremner, Charlton, Hunter, Greenhoff, Lorimer, Storrie, Giles, O'Grady

1966/67   INTER-CITIES FAIRS CUP

FIRST ROUND

Leeds United received a bye to the second round

SECOND ROUND First Leg
DWS Amsterdam 1 Leeds United 3 (Bremner, Johanneson, Greenhoff)
Sprake, Reaney, Bell, Bremner, Charlton, Hunter, O'Grady, Greenhoff, Madeley, Giles, Johanneson

SECOND ROUND Second Leg
Leeds United 5 (Johanneson 3, Giles, Madeley) DWS Amsterdam 1
Sprake, Reaney, Bell, Bremner, Charlton, Hunter, Storrie, Madeley, Greenhoff, Giles, Johanneson

Leeds United win on aggregate 8-2

THIRD ROUND First Leg
Leeds United 1 (Greenhoff) Valencia 1
Sprake, Reaney, Madeley, Bremner, Charlton, Hunter, Giles, Gray E., Greenhoff, Collins, Cooper

THIRD ROUND Second Leg
Valencia 0 Leeds United 2 (Giles, Lorimer)
Sprake, Madeley, Bell, Bremner, Charlton, Hunter, Giles, Lorimer, Belfitt, Gray E., Hibbitt

Leeds United win on aggregate 3-1

QUARTER-FINAL First Leg
Bologna 1 Leeds United 0
Sprake, Reaney, Bell, Bremner, Charlton, Hunter, Lorimer, Belfitt, Madeley, Giles, Cooper

QUARTER-FINAL Second Leg
Leeds United 1 (Giles) Bologna 0
Sprake, Reaney, Bell, Bremner, Madeley, Hunter, Giles, Belfitt, Greenhoff, Gray E., Cooper

Leeds United win on toss of a disc after drawing on aggregate 1-1

SEMI-FINAL First Leg
Leeds United 4 (Belfitt 3, Giles) Kilmarnock 2
Sprake, Reaney, Bell, Bremner, Madeley, Hunter, O'Grady, Lorimer, Belfitt, Giles, Gray E.

SEMI-FINAL Second Leg
Kilmarnock 0 Leeds United 0
Sprake, Reaney, Bell, Bremner, Madeley, Hunter, Lorimer, Gray E., Belfitt, Giles, Cooper

Leeds United win on aggregate 4-2

FINAL First Leg
Dinamo Zagreb 2 Leeds United 0
Sprake, Reaney, Cooper, Bremner, Charlton, Hunter, Bates, Lorimer, Belfitt, Gray E., O'Grady

FINAL Second Leg
Leeds United 0 Dinamo Zagreb 0
Sprake, Reaney, Bell, Bremner, Charlton, Hunter, Cooper, Belfitt, Greenhoff, Giles, O'Grady

Dinamo Zagreb win on aggregate 2-0

1967/68   INTER-CITIES FAIRS CUP

FIRST ROUND First Leg
CA Spora 0 Leeds United 9 (Lorimer 4, Bremner, Greenhoff 2, Madeley, Jones)
Harvey, Reaney, Madeley, Bremner, Charlton, Hunter, Greenhoff, Lorimer, Jones, Gray E., Cooper

FIRST ROUND Second Leg
Leeds United 7 (Johanneson 3, Greenhoff 2, Cooper, Lorimer) CA Spora 0
Sprake, Reaney, Cooper, Madeley (Bates), Charlton, Hunter, Greenhoff, Lorimer, Belfitt, Hibbitt, Johanneson

Leeds United win on aggregate 16-0

SECOND ROUND First Leg
Partizan Belgrade 1 Leeds United 2 (Lorimer, Belfitt)
Harvey, Reaney, Cooper, Bremner, Charlton, Hunter, Greenhoff, Lorimer, Madeley, Belfitt, Gray E. (Bates)

SECOND ROUND Second Leg
Leeds United 1 (Lorimer) Partizan Belgrade 1
Sprake, Reaney, Cooper, Bremner, Charlton, Hunter, Greenhoff, Lorimer, Madeley, Gray E., Hibbitt (Johanneson)

Leeds United win on aggregate 3-2

THIRD ROUND First Leg
Leeds United 1 (Gray E.) Hibernian 0
Sprake, Reaney (Madeley), Cooper, Bremner, Charlton, Hunter, Greenhoff, Lorimer, Jones, Giles, Gray E.

THIRD ROUND Second Leg
Hibernian 1 Leeds United 1 (Charlton)
Sprake, Reaney, Cooper, Bremner, Charlton, Hunter, Greenhoff, Lorimer, Jones, Giles, Gray E.

Leeds United win on aggregate 2-1

QUARTER-FINAL First Leg
Rangers 0 Leeds United 0
Sprake, Reaney, Cooper, Bremner, Charlton, Hunter, Greenhoff (Belfitt), Lorimer, Jones, Giles, Madeley

QUARTER-FINAL Second Leg
Leeds United 2 (Giles, Lorimer) Rangers 0
Harvey, Reaney, Cooper, Bremner, Charlton, Hunter, Greenhoff, Lorimer, Jones, Giles, Madeley

Leeds United win on aggregate 2-0

SEMI-FINAL First Leg
Dundee 1 Leeds United 1 (Madeley)
Harvey, Reaney, Cooper, Bremner, Charlton, Hunter, Greenhoff, Lorimer, Madeley, Giles, Gray E.

SEMI-FINAL Second Leg
Leeds United 1 (Gray E.) Dundee 0
Sprake, Reaney, Cooper, Bremner, Madeley, Hunter, Greenhoff, Lorimer, Jones, Giles, Gray E.

Leeds United win on aggregate 2-1

FINAL First Leg
Leeds United 1 (Jones) Ferencvaros 0
Sprake, Reaney, Cooper, Bremner, Charlton, Hunter, Lorimer, Madeley, Jones (Belfitt), Giles (Greenhoff), Gray E.

FINAL Second Leg
Ferencvaros 0 Leeds United 0
Sprake, Reaney, Cooper, Bremner, Charlton, Hunter, O'Grady, Lorimer, Jones, Madeley, Hibbitt (Bates)

Leeds United win on aggregate 1-0

1968/69   INTER-CITIES FAIRS CUP

FIRST ROUND First Leg
Standard Liege 0 Leeds United 0
Sprake, Reaney, Cooper, Bremner, Charlton, Hunter, O'Grady, Lorimer, Jones, Madeley, Hibbitt

FIRST ROUND Second Leg
Leeds United 3 (Charlton, Lorimer, Bremner) Standard Liege 2
Sprake, Reaney, Cooper (Bates), Bremner, Charlton, Hunter, O'Grady, Lorimer, Jones, Madeley, Hibbitt (Gray E.)

Leeds United win on aggregate 3-2

SECOND ROUND First Leg
Leeds United 2 (Charlton 2) Naples 0
Sprake, Reaney, Madeley, Bremner, Charlton, Hunter, Lorimer, Belfitt, Jones, Giles, O'Grady

SECOND ROUND Second Leg
Naples 2 Leeds United 0
Sprake, Reaney, Cooper, Bremner, Charlton, Hunter, O'Grady, Madeley, Jones, Giles, Gray E.

Leeds United win on toss of a disc after drawing on aggregate 2-2

THIRD ROUND First Leg
Leeds United 5 (O'Grady, Hunter, Lorimer 2, Charlton) Hannover 1
Sprake, Reaney, Madeley, Bremner, Charlton, Hunter, O'Grady (Hibbitt), Lorimer, Jones, Giles, Gray E.

THIRD ROUND Second Leg
Hannover 1 Leeds United 2 (Belfitt, Jones)
Sprake, Reaney, Cooper, Bremner, Charlton, Hunter, O'Grady, Lorimer, Jones, Belfitt, Gray E.

Leeds United win on aggregate 7-2

QUARTER-FINAL First Leg
Leeds United 0 Ujpest Dosza 1
Sprake, Reaney, Madeley, Bremner, Charlton, Hunter, O'Grady, Belfitt (Lorimer), Jones, Giles, Gray E.

QUARTER-FINAL Second Leg
Ujpest Dosza 2 Leeds United 0
Sprake, Bates, Cooper, Bremner, Madeley, Hunter, Lorimer (Yorath), Belfitt, Jones (Hibbitt), Giles, Gray E.

Ujpest Dosza win on aggregate 3-0

1969/70   EUROPEAN CUP

FIRST ROUND First Leg
Leeds United 10 (Jones 3, Clarke 2, Bremner 2, Giles 2, O'Grady) Lyn Oslo 0
Sprake, Reaney, Cooper, Bremner, Charlton, Hunter, Madeley, Clarke, Jones, Giles (Bates), O'Grady

FIRST ROUND Second Leg
Lyn Oslo 0 Leeds United 6 (Hibbitt 2, Belfitt 2, Jones, Lorimer)
Sprake, Reaney, Cooper, Bremner, Madeley, Gray E., Lorimer, Belfitt, Jones, Bates, Hibbitt

Leeds United win on aggregate 16-0

SECOND ROUND First Leg
Leeds United 3 (Jones 2, Giles) Ferencvaros 0
Sprake, Reaney, Madeley, Bremner, Charlton, Hunter, Lorimer, Bates, Jones, Giles, Gray E.

SECOND ROUND Second Leg
Ferencvaros 0 Leeds United 3 (Jones 2, Lorimer)
Sprake, Reaney, Cooper, Bremner, Charlton, Hunter, Lorimer, Madeley, Jones, Giles, Gray E. (Galvin)

Leeds United win on aggregate 6-0

QUARTER-FINAL First Leg
Standard Liege 0 Leeds United 1 (Lorimer)
Sprake, Reaney, Cooper, Bremner, Charlton, Hunter, Lorimer, Clarke, Jones, Giles, Madeley

QUARTER-FINAL Second Leg
Leeds United 1 (Giles) Standard Liege 0
Sprake, Reaney, Cooper, Bremner, Charlton, Hunter, Lorimer, Clarke, Jones, Giles, Madeley

Leeds United win on aggregate 2-0

SEMI-FINAL First Leg
Leeds United 0 Celtic 1
Sprake, Reaney, Cooper, Bremner (Bates), Charlton, Madeley, Lorimer, Clarke, Jones, Giles, Gray E.

SEMI-FINAL Second Leg
Celtic 2 Leeds United 1 (Bremner)
Sprake (Harvey), Madeley, Cooper, Bremner, Charlton, Hunter, Lorimer (Bates), Clarke, Jones, Giles, Gray E.

Celtic win on aggregate 3-1

1970/71   UEFA CUP

FIRST ROUND First Leg
Sarpsborg 0 Leeds United 1 (Lorimer)
Sprake, Madeley, Cooper, Bremner, Kennedy, Gray E., Lorimer, Belfitt, Jones, Bates, Hibbitt

FIRST ROUND Second Leg
Leeds United 5 (Charlton 2, Bremner 2, Lorimer) Sarpsborg 0
Sprake, Madeley, Cooper (Reaney), Bremner, Charlton, Hunter, Lorimer, Clarke, Belfitt, Bates, Gray E.

Leeds United win on aggregate 6-0

SECOND ROUND First Leg
Leeds United 1 (Lorimer) Dinamo Dresden 0
Harvey, Davey, Cooper, Bremner, Charlton, Hunter, Lorimer, Clarke, Jones, Belfitt (Galvin), Madeley

SECOND ROUND Second Leg
Dinamo Dresden 2 Leeds United 1 (Jones)
Sprake, Davey, Madeley, Bremner, Charlton, Hunter, Lorimer, Clarke, Jones, Giles, Bates

Leeds United win on away goals rule after 2-2 draw on aggregate

THIRD ROUND First Leg
Leeds United 6 (Clarke, Bremner, Gray E. 2, Charlton, Chovanec o.g.) Sparta Prague 0
Sprake, Madeley, Cooper, Bremner, Charlton, Hunter, Lorimer, Clarke, Belfitt (Reaney), Giles, Gray E.

THIRD ROUND Second Leg
Sparta Prague 2 Leeds United 3 (Clarke, Belfitt, Gray E.)
Sprake (Harvey), Reaney, Cooper, Bremner, Madeley, Hunter (Yorath), Lorimer, Clarke, Belfitt, Bates, Gray E.

Leeds United win on aggregate 9-2

QUARTER-FINAL First Leg
Leeds United 2 (Lorimer, Giles) Vitoria Setubal 1
Harvey, Davey (Yorath), Reaney, Bates, Charlton, Hunter, Lorimer, Belfitt, Jones (Jordan), Giles, Madeley

QUARTER-FINAL Second Leg
Vitoria Setubal 1 Leeds United 1 (Lorimer)
Harvey (Sprake), Reaney, Cooper, Bates, Charlton, Hunter, Lorimer, Clarke, Jones, Giles, Madeley

Leeds United win on aggregate 3-2

SEMI-FINAL First Leg
Liverpool 0 Leeds United 1 (Bremner)
Sprake, Reaney (Davey), Cooper, Bremner, Charlton, Hunter, Bates, Clarke, Jones, Giles, Madeley

SEMI-FINAL Second Leg
Leeds United 0 Liverpool 0
Sprake, Madeley, Cooper, Bremner, Charlton, Hunter, Bates, Clarke (Reaney), Jones (Jordan), Giles, Gray E.

Leeds United win on aggregate 1-0

FINAL First Leg
Juventus 2 Leeds United 2 (Madeley, Bates)
Sprake, Reaney, Cooper, Bremner, Charlton, Hunter, Lorimer, Clarke, Jones (Bates), Giles, Madeley

Match originally played was abandoned after 56 minutes due to a waterlogged pitch, score at time 0-0

FINAL Second Leg
Leeds United 1 (Clarke) Juventus 1
Sprake, Reaney, Cooper, Bremner, Charlton, Hunter, Lorimer, Clarke, Jones, Giles, Madeley (Bates)

Leeds United win on away-goals rule after 3-3 draw on aggregate

INTER-CITIES FAIRS CUP PLAY-OFF

Barcelona 2 Leeds United 1 (Jordan)
Sprake, Reaney, Davey, Bremner, Charlton, Hunter, Lorimer, Jordan, Belfitt, Giles, Galvin

This match between the first and last winners of the Inter-Cities Fairs Cup was played to decide who would keep the trophy forever.

1971/72   UEFA CUP

FIRST ROUND First Leg
Lierse SK 0 Leeds United 2 (Galvin, Lorimer)
Sprake, Reaney, Yorath, Bremner, Faulkner, Hunter, Lorimer, Galvin, Belfitt, Giles, Bates

FIRST ROUND Second Leg
Leeds United 0 Lierse SK 4
Shaw (Sprake), Reaney, Cooper, Yorath, Faulkner, Madeley, Lorimer, Mann (Hunter), Belfitt, Bates, Galvin

Lierse win on aggregate 4-2

1972/73   EUROPEAN CUP WINNERS' CUP

FIRST ROUND First Leg
Ankaragucu 1 Leeds United 1 (Jordan)
Harvey, Reaney, Cherry, Bremner, Ellam, Hunter, Lorimer, Galvin (Yorath), Jordan, Giles, Madeley

FIRST ROUND Second Leg
Leeds United 1 (Jones) Ankaragucu 0
Harvey, Reaney, Cherry, Bremner, Ellam, Hunter, Lorimer, Clarke, Jones, Giles, Bates

Leeds United win on aggregate 2-1

SECOND ROUND First Leg
Carl Zeiss Jena 0 Leeds United 0
Harvey, Madeley, Cherry, Bremner, Charlton, Hunter, Lorimer, Clarke, Jordan, Bates, Gray E.

SECOND ROUND Second Leg
Leeds United 2 (Cherry, Jones) Carl Zeiss Jena 0
Harvey, Reaney, Cherry, Bremner, Charlton, Hunter, Lorimer, Clarke, Jones, Bates (Giles), Yorath

Leeds United win 2-0 on aggregate

QUARTER-FINAL First Leg
Leeds United 5 (Giles, Clarke, Lorimer 2, Jordan) Rapid Bucharest 0
Harvey, Reaney, Cherry, Bremner, McQueen (Yorath), Hunter, Lorimer, Clarke, Jordan, Giles, Madeley

QUARTER-FINAL Second Leg
Rapid Bucharest 1 Leeds United 3 (Bates, Jones, Jordan)
Harvey, Reaney, Gray E., Madeley, McQueen, Hunter, Lorimer, Jordan, Jones, Giles (Yorath), Bates (Gray F.)

Leeds United win on aggregate 8-1

SEMI-FINAL First Leg
Leeds United 1 (Clarke) Hajduk Split 0
Harvey, Reaney, Cherry, Bremner, Yorath, Hunter, Lorimer, Clarke, Jones, Giles, Bates (Jordan)

SEMI-FINAL Second Leg
Hajduk Split 0 Leeds United 0
Harvey, Reaney, Cherry, Bremner, Yorath, Hunter, Lorimer, Jordan, Jones, Giles, Madeley

Leeds United win on aggregate 1-0

FINAL *in Salonika, Greece*
AC Milan 1 Leeds United 0
Harvey, Reaney, Cherry, Bates, Yorath, Hunter, Lorimer, Jordan, Jones, Gray F. (McQueen), Madeley

1973/74   UEFA CUP

FIRST ROUND First Leg
Stromsgodset 1 Leeds United 1 (Clarke)
Sprake, Madeley, Cherry, Yorath, McQueen, Gray F., Liddell, Clarke, Jones, Bates, Gray E.

FIRST ROUND Second Leg
Leeds United 6 (Clarke 2, Jones 2, Gray F., Bates) Stromsgodset 1
Harvey, Reaney (O'Neil), Cherry, Bremner, Ellam, Yorath, Lorimer, Clarke (McGinley), Jones, Bates, Gray F.

Leeds United win on aggregate 7-2

SECOND ROUND First Leg
Leeds United 0 Hibernian 0
Harvey, Madeley, Cherry, Bremner, Ellam, Yorath, Lorimer, Clarke, Jones (Jordan), Bates, Gray F.

SECOND ROUND Second Leg
Hibernian 0 Leeds United 0
Shaw (Letheren), Reaney, Cherry, Bremner, Ellam, Yorath, Lorimer, Clarke, Jordan, Bates, Gray F.

Leeds United win on penalties 5-4 after 0-0 draw on aggregate

THIRD ROUND First Leg
Leeds United 1 (Cherry) Vitoria Setubal 0
Harvey, Reaney (Davey), Cherry, Bremner, McQueen, Hunter, Lorimer, Clarke, Jordan, Bates, Yorath, (Gray F.)

THIRD ROUND Second Leg
Vitoria Setubal 3 Leeds United 1 (Liddell)
Harvey, Reaney, Cherry, Yorath, McQueen (Liddell), Ellam, Lorimer, Mann, Jordan, Hampton, Gray F.

Vitoria Setubal win on aggregate 3-2

1974/75   EUROPEAN CUP

FIRST ROUND First Leg
Leeds United 4 (Clarke 2, Lorimer, Jordan) FC Zurich 1
Harvey, Reaney, Cooper, Yorath, McQueen, Hunter, Lorimer, Clarke, Jordan, Giles, Madeley

FIRST ROUND Second Leg
FC Zurich 2 Leeds United 1 (Clarke)
Harvey, Reaney, Cherry, Yorath, Madeley, Hunter, Lorimer, Clarke, Jordan, Bates, Gray F. (Hampton)

Leeds United win on aggregate 5-3

SECOND ROUND First Leg
Ujpest Dosza 1 Leeds United 2 (Lorimer, McQueen)
Harvey, Reaney, Cooper, Yorath, McQueen, Hunter, Lorimer, McKenzie, Jordan, Giles, Madeley

SECOND ROUND Second Leg
Leeds United 3 (McQueen, Bremner, Yorath) Ujpest Dosza 0
Harvey, Reaney, Cooper, Yorath, McQueen, Hunter (Cherry), Lorimer (Harris), Clarke, Bremner, Giles, Madeley

Leeds United win on aggregate 5-1

QUARTER-FINAL First Leg
Leeds United 3 (Jordan, McQueen, Lorimer) Anderlecht 0
Stewart, Madeley, Gray F., Bremner (Yorath), McQueen, Hunter, Lorimer, Clarke, Jordan, Giles, Gray E.

QUARTER-FINAL Second Leg
Anderlecht 0 Leeds United 1 (Bremner)
Stewart, Reaney, Gray F., Bremner, McQueen, Hunter, Lorimer, Clarke, Jordan, Yorath, Madeley

Leeds United win on aggregate 4-0

SEMI-FINAL First Leg
Leeds United 2 (Bremner, Clarke) Barcelona 1
Stewart, Reaney, Gray F., Bremner, McQueen, Madeley, Yorath, Clarke, Jordan, Giles, Gray E.

SEMI-FINAL Second Leg
Barcelona 1 Leeds United 1 (Lorimer)
Stewart, Cherry, Gray F., Bremner, McQueen, Hunter, Lorimer, Clarke, Jordan, Yorath, Madeley

Leeds United win on aggregate 3-2

FINAL *in Paris, France*
Bayern Munich 2 Leeds United 0
Stewart, Reaney, Gray F., Bremner, Madeley, Hunter, Lorimer, Clarke, Jordan, Giles, Yorath (Gray E.)

1979/80   UEFA CUP

FIRST ROUND First Leg
Valetta 0 Leeds United 4 (Graham 3, Hart)
Harvey, Hird, Hampton, Flynn, Hart, Madeley, Gray E., Cherry, Hankin, Curtis, Graham (Harris)

FIRST ROUND Second Leg
Leeds United 3 (Hart, Hankin, Curtis) Valetta 0
Lukic, Hird, Hampton, Flynn, Hart, Parkinson, Hamson, Cherry, Hankin, Curtis, Graham

Leeds United win on aggregate 7-0

SECOND ROUND First Leg
Universitatea Craiova 2 Leeds United 0
Lukic, Hird, Stevenson, Flynn, Hart, Madeley, Harris (Hamson), Cherry, Hankin, Curtis, Gray E.

SECOND ROUND Second Leg
Leeds United 0 Universitatea Craiova 2
Lukic, Cherry, Stevenson, Flynn, Hart, Madeley, Gray E., Parkinson (Harris), Hankin, Curtis, Graham

Universitatea Craiova win on aggregate 4-0

1992/93 EUROPEAN CUP

FIRST ROUND First Leg
VFB Stuttgart 3 Leeds United 0
Lukic, Rocastle (Hodge), Dorigo, Batty, Fairclough, Whyte, Cantona (Shutt), Strachan, Chapman, McAllister, Speed

FIRST ROUND Second Leg
Leeds United 4 (Speed, McAllister, Cantona, Chapman) VFB Stuttgart 1
Lukic, Sellers, Dorigo, Batty, Fairclough, Whyte, Strachan, Cantona, Chapman, McAllister, Speed

VFB Stuttgart win on away goals rule after 4-4 draw on aggregate, but UEFA ruled that a play-off match must be played after VFB Stuttgart found guilty of breaking the foreign player rule.

FIRST ROUND PLAY-OFF
Leeds United 2 (Strachan, Shutt) VFB Stuttgart 1
Lukic, Newsome, Dorigo, Batty, Fairclough, Whyte, Strachan, Cantona (Shutt), Chapman, McAllister, Speed

SECOND ROUND First Leg
Rangers 2 Leeds United 1 (McAllister)
Lukic, Newsome, Dorigo, Batty, Fairclough, Whyte, Strachan (Rocastle), Cantona (Rod Wallace), Chapman, McAllister, Speed

SECOND ROUND Second Leg
Leeds United 1 (Cantona) Rangers 2
Lukic, Newsome, Dorigo, Rocastle (Hodge), Fairclough (Rod Wallace), Whyte, Strachan, Cantona, Chapman, McAllister, Speed

Rangers win on aggregate 4-2

1995/96 UEFA CUP

FIRST ROUND First Leg
AS Monaco 0 Leeds United 3 (Yeboah 3)
Lukic, Kelly, Dorigo (Beesley), Palmer, Wetherall, Pemberton, Whelan, Yeboah, Deane, McAllister, Speed

FIRST ROUND Second Leg
Leeds United 0 AS Monaco 1
Lukic, Kelly, Beesley, Palmer, Wetherall, Pemberton (Couzens), White (Tinkler), Yeboah, Deane, McAllister, Speed

Leeds United win on aggregate 3-1

SECOND ROUND First Leg
Leeds United 3 (Palmer, McAllister, Speed) PSV Eindhoven 5
Lukic, Kelly, Dorigo (Beesley), Palmer, Wetherall, Pemberton, Whelan (Wallace), Yeboah, Deane, McAllister, Speed (Couzens)

SECOND ROUND Second Leg
PSV Eindhoven 3 Leeds United 0
Lukic, Kelly, Beesley (Ford), Palmer, Wetherall, Pemberton, Whelan (White), Yeboah, Bowman, McAllister, Speed (Sharp)

PSV Eindhoven win on aggregate 8-3

1998/99   UEFA CUP

FIRST ROUND First Leg
Leeds United 1 (Hasselbaink) CS Maritimo 0
Martyn, Halle, Harte, Hopkin, Radebe, Molenaar, Hiden, Kewell (Sharpe), Hasselbaink, Ribeiro (Haaland), Bowyer

FIRST ROUND Second Leg
CS Maritimo 1 Leeds United 0

Leeds United win on penalties 4-1 after 1-1 draw on aggregate

SECOND ROUND First Leg
AS Roma 1 Leeds United 0
Robinson, Granville, Hiden, Hopkin (Haaland), Radebe, Woodgate, Molenaar, Kewell, Hasselbaink (Wijnhard), McPhail, Bowyer

SECOND ROUND Second Leg
Leeds United 0 AS Roma 0
Martyn, Woodgate, Harte, Hopkin, Wetherall (Wijnhard), Molenaar, Hiden, Kewell, Hasselbaink, McPhail (Haaland), Bowyer

AS Roma win on aggregate 1-0

1999/2000   UEFA CUP

FIRST ROUND First Leg
Partizan Belgrade 1 Leeds United 3 (Bowyer 2, Radebe)
Martyn, Kelly, Harte, Batty, Radebe, Woodgate, Hopkin, Bridges (Smith), Mills, Kewell, Bowyer

FIRST ROUND Second Leg
Leeds United 1 (Huckerby) Partizan Belgrade 0
Martyn, Kelly, Harte, Batty, Woodgate, Radebe, Hopkin (Bakke), Bridges (Smith), Huckerby, Kewell (Jones), Bowyer

Leeds United win on aggregate 4-1

SECOND ROUND First Leg
Leeds United 4 (Bowyer 2, Smith, Kewell) Lokomotiv Moscow 1
Martyn, Kelly, Harte, Batty, Woodgate, Radebe, McPhail, Bridges (Huckerby), Smith, Kewell (Jones), Bowyer

SECOND ROUND Second Leg
Lokomotiv Moscow 0 Leeds United 3 (Bridges 2, Harte)
Martyn, Kelly, Harte, Batty, Woodgate, Radebe, McPhail (Hopkin), Bridges, Bakke, Kewell (Huckerby), Bowyer (Haaland)

Leeds United win on aggregate 7-1

THIRD ROUND First Leg
Spartak Moscow 2 Leeds United 1 (Kewell)
Martyn, Kelly, Harte, Haaland, Woodgate, Duberry, McPhail, Bridges (Huckerby), Bakke, Kewell, Bowyer

THIRD ROUND Second Leg
Leeds United 1 (Radebe) Spartak Moscow 0
Martyn, Kelly, Harte, Bakke, Woodgate, Radebe, McPhail, Bridges, Smith (Huckerby), Kewell, Bowyer

Leeds United win on away goals rule after 2-2 draw on aggregate

FOURTH ROUND First Leg
AS Roma 0 Leeds United 0
Martyn, Kelly, Harte, Haaland, Woodgate, Radebe, Jones, Bridges (Smith), Bakke, Kewell, Bowyer

FOURTH ROUND Second Leg
Leeds United 1 (Kewell) AS Roma 0
Martyn, Kelly, Harte, Bakke (Jones), Radebe, Haaland, McPhail (Huckerby), Bridges (Smith), Wilcox, Kewell, Bowyer

Leeds United win on aggregate 1-0

QUARTER-FINAL First Leg
Leeds United 3 (Wilcox, Kewell, Bowyer) Slavia Prague 0
Martyn, Kelly, Harte, Bakke, Radebe, Haaland, McPhail (Huckerby), Bridges (Smith), Wilcox, Kewell, Bowyer

QUARTER-FINAL Second Leg
Slavia Prague 2 Leeds United 1 (Kewell)
Martyn, Kelly, Harte, Haaland, Radebe, Woodgate, McPhail, Bridges (Smith), Bakke, Kewell, Jones

Leeds United win on aggregate 4-2

SEMI-FINAL First Leg
Galatasaray 2 Leeds United 0
Martyn, Kelly, Harte, Jones (Wilcox), Radebe, Woodgate, McPhail, Bridges (Huckerby), Bakke, Kewell, Bowyer

SEMI-FINAL Second Leg
Leeds United 2 (Bakke 2) Galatasaray 2
Martyn, Mills, Harte (Huckerby), Wilcox, Radebe, Woodgate, McPhail, Bridges, Bakke, Kewell, Bowyer

Galatasaray win on aggregate 4-2

Acknowledgements

The authors would like to thank *The Yorkshire Post Newspapers Ltd* for supplying the majority of images for this book. We would also like to thank the following people and organisations for their help with this publication: former players Mick Jones and Paul Madeley; Leeds United Football Club; Mike Fisher; David Hartshorne and Keith Hampshire at *The Yorkshire Post Newspapers Ltd*; Jack Hickes of Photographers Ltd; Tony Lazenby; and James Howarth at Tempus Publishing.